Companions in Crime

The Social Aspects of Criminal Conduct

Criminologists often allude to "peer influence" in explanations of crime and delinquency, but the meaning of that concept rarely receives careful attention. *Companions in Crime* organizes the extensive literature on peer influence and group delinquency into a coherent form for the first time. Chapters focus on the role of peers over the life course, the group nature of delinquent behavior, and the applicability of peer influence for explaining the major features of delinquent behavior. The most extensive chapter of the book examines possible mechanisms of peer influence and the evidence in favor of each. The principal thesis of *Companions in Crime* is that deviant behavior is predominantly social behavior and that criminologists must eventually determine the significance of that fact.

Mark Warr is Professor of Sociology at the University of Texas at Austin. He is the author of nearly fifty publications on crime and delinquency and has served on numerous national commissions and panels for agencies such as the National Academy of Sciences, the National Science Foundation, and the National Institute of Justice. He also has served on the editorial boards of the *American Sociological Review*, the *American Journal of Sociology*, and *Criminology* and is a recipient of the President's Associates Teaching Excellence Award.

D1018893

Cambridge Studies in Criminology

Edited by
Alfred Blumstein, *H. John Heinz School of Public Policy and Management, Carnegie Mellon University*
David Farrington, *Institute of Criminology, University of Cambridge*

Other books in the series:

Companions in Crime

The Social Aspects of Criminal Conduct

Mark Warr
University of Texas at Austin

PUBLISHED BY THE PRESS SYNDICATE OF THE UNIVERSITY OF CAMBRIDGE
The Pitt Building, Trumpington Street, Cambridge, United Kingdom

CAMBRIDGE UNIVERSITY PRESS
The Edinburgh Building, Cambridge CB2 2RU, UK
40 West 20th Street, New York, NY 10011-4211, USA
10 Stamford Road, Oakleigh, VIC 3166, Australia
Ruiz de Alarcón 13, 28014 Madrid, Spain
Dock House, The Waterfront, Cape Town 8001, South Africa

http://www.cambridge.org

First published 2002

Printed in the United States of America

Typeface ITC New Baskerville 10/14 pt.   *System* LaTeX 2_ε [TB]

A catalog record for this book is available from the British Library.

Library of Congress Cataloging in Publication data
Warr, Mark, 1952–
Companions in crime : the social aspects of criminal conduct / Mark Warr.
p.   cm. – (Cambridge studies in criminology)
Includes bibliographical references and index.
ISBN 0-521-81083-3 – ISBN 0-521-00916-2 (pb.)
1. Criminal behavior – Social aspects.   2. Peer pressure.   3. Social groups.
I. Title.   II. Cambridge studies in criminology (New York, N.Y.)
HV6155.W37 2002
364.2'5 – dc21   2001037395

ISBN 0 521 81083 3 hardback
ISBN 0 521 00916 2 paperback

Contents

Preface

This book is a mixture of the old and the new, of ideas that took root in me as a young man and those that have steered my research in more recent years. It is a book that brings together questions that intrigued criminologists decades ago with ones that hold center stage today in the field of criminology.

As a graduate student at the University of Arizona in the middle and late 1970s, I was privileged to work with a group of faculty members that included Maynard Erickson, Jack Gibbs, and Gary Jensen. Their joint research concentrated on the deterrent effect of legal sanctions, but unlike many others working on the issue at the time, they conceived of the topic in a broad sociological sense. How much does the public know about the criminal sanctions prescribed by law, and how can sanctions deter those who are unaware of them? How does one measure the severity of a legal punishment, and how does the objective severity of a punishment (say, years spent in prison) correspond to its perceived severity? Do public perceptions of crime (e.g., the relative incidence of different offenses) and of punishment (e.g., the conditional probability of arrest) accord with reality? Only later was I to realize how truly original and prescient much of this work was. But the mutual interest of these investigators in the social psychology of crime and punishment was to stimulate one persisting line of research in my own career.

Maynard Erickson's interest in deterrence was connected with an-other of his long-standing concerns, the group nature of delinquent behavior. Certain questions about the social character of delinquency fascinated him. Does offending in a group affect one's chances of be-ing caught by the police? How are criminological data (particularly self-report and official data) affected by the group nature of offend-ing? If the causes of delinquency are to be found in groups, does the cure lie there as well?

At the time, I remained largely unimpressed by questions like these (or so I thought), but some of the issues raised by Maynard simmered in the back of my mind for years afterward. They grew more pressing as I taught courses in criminology to hundreds of students at Penn-sylvania State University and the University of Texas. Teaching a large field in a short period of time forces one to make decisions about what is and what is not important to a field. At the same time, many crim-inologists in the 1980s and 1990s were returning to first principles by reexamining old but essential questions: Why are the young more inclined toward crime than the old? Why are females so much less susceptible to criminal behavior than males? With time, I too became preoccupied with the sorts of foundational questions that Maynard had inspired in me, and that still preoccupy me today. Does the group nature of delinquency tell us anything about its causes? When one hears of "peer influence," what exactly does that mean? How can it be demonstrated?

Aside from my professional training, some of my interest in peer influence no doubt stems from my own biography. As a youth, I spent a great deal of time with others my age. For years I was busy as a musician, a collective occupation if ever there was one, and one that requires many hours spent with others in practice, traveling, and performance. Occasionally my activities with friends strayed into the criminal, and I still marvel at some of my own behavior from those days. I recall how intensely I wanted to belong to certain groups, and how the legality of our behavior rarely entered our minds – we simply did what "we" wanted to do. I also remember, however, that there were real self-imposed limits on what I would do, though I often did things not of my own choosing simply to avoid the rejection or rebuke of my companions. In time, I came to realize that I rarely did the same things *outside* the group that I did *inside* the group, a fact that struck me even then. Today, many years later, it still surprises me to recall how, when my teenage years had come to a close, I simply walked away from many of the friends who had once mattered greatly to me. Their life plans or lifestyles no longer matched mine, and I was already looking forward to marriage and a career.

As a scholar, the twists and turns in my own intellectual path have intersected with developments in the field of criminology itself. One of those developments has been the widespread adoption of the life-course perspective (see Elder, 1985) by criminologists. Briefly, the life-course perspective concentrates on changes in criminality *within* individual biographies as persons progress from childhood through old age and experience (or do not experience) major life-course transitions like marriage, higher education, full-time employment, and parenthood. It also explores the intersection of biography and history as members of a society experience common events (war, depression, an election), but at quite different stages in the life course.

The life-course perspective is well suited to the study of peer influence because most aspects of peer relations (e.g., time spent with peers, susceptibility to peer influence) are highly age-dependent phenomena. In fact, systemic changes in patterns of peer interaction are one of the hallmarks of the phase of life we call adolescence. By examining peer relations in their proper developmental and social context, one can hope to better understand their origins and progression and, ultimately, their link to another highly age-dependent phenomenon – criminal behavior.

Another development in criminology that has influenced my work has been the gradual secession of criminology from the field of sociology. The reasons for this rift are complex, but they include, I think, the general indifference of some sociologists toward the study of crime and deviance, and the eagerness of many universities to exploit the explosive demand among students for courses and degrees that have the word "crime" in them. Many universities have created entirely new programs, departments, and degrees around the topic for reasons that make little intellectual sense and that inspire little confidence in the integrity of administrators. My own concern with this issue has less to do with changing institutional arrangements and disciplinary boundaries than with the intellectual implications of this schism for the study of crime. As I find myself constantly reminding students, criminal behavior is human behavior, and human behavior has been the object of scientific study at least since the time of Comte. One cannot simply divorce the study of crime from other domains of human behavior, or ignore the collective knowledge and progress of the social sciences. Most of the concepts and arguments of criminology have their roots in other disciplines (consider the life-course perspective as one example), and if criminologists fail to expose their students to the core disciplines of the social sciences, the long-term consequences could be catastrophic. As a criminologist who is first and foremost a sociologist, I cannot overstate the advantages that a sociological foundation has brought to my understanding of crime, and I hope that this book is in some small way testimony to its value.

As this book has taken form, I have come to think of its structure as something like a pyramid. The first three chapters are logically preliminary to the fourth, and the remaining chapters are applications or elaborations of preceding chapters. I urge readers to follow the progression of the book if at all possible, or at least to read the material on adolescence before proceeding to theories of peer influence. A few portions of the book have been adapted from earlier work of mine, primarily articles appearing in journals of sociology and criminology. This is especially true of Chapter 5, but only occasionally elsewhere. I beg the indulgence of those who have encountered some of this material before; its relevance is obvious.

Perhaps the most difficult aspect of writing about peer influence is that existing empirical evidence on the matter, while plentiful, can be construed in different – and sometimes quite contradictory – ways. Some investigators dismiss evidence of peer influence without a second thought, whereas others see a compelling case for peer influence as a causal agent in criminal behavior. My objectives in this book have been to offer an informed assessment of the evidence, and to build the case for how such influence might work. Beneath these goals lies the hope that criminologists will concentrate their attention on the issue with

the aim of resolving the question one way or the other. Outside the
social sciences, it is rare for an explanation to be so promising while
the question remains unsettled for so long. Surely the mark of an
advanced science is an ability to achieve at least moderate consensus on
empirical questions within a reasonable period of time. The question
of peer influence in criminology is now almost a century old. That is
time enough.

Acknowledgments

This book is dedicated to those who have supported and guided my life-long quest to understand human behavior, especially those behaviors that cross legal and moral boundaries. Jack P. Gibbs is the most genuinely intelligent person I have ever encountered, and he taught me to respect language and logic and to pursue questions and arguments to their ends. From him I learned to appreciate social phenomena – which are often unobserved or unobservable – as real, measurable, and consequential things.

Like Jack, Otis Dudley Duncan impressed on me the nobility of reason, and he taught me the craft of extracting order and sense from recalcitrant social data. Dudley's life and work give meaning to the term erudition, and I suspect that few human beings have ever more fully appreciated the connections among the sciences, the arts, and the humanities.

In his office and after hours, Maynard L. Erickson conveyed to me the raw excitement of ideas, and he more than any other person alerted me to the social nature of deviant behavior. Gary F. Jensen taught me to respect the intellectual traditions of my own field, and how to combine a professional and a moral life. James F. Short, a gentle man loved by many, has been a father figure to me throughout my career. Not only is he a bridge between generations of scholars, but in the sciences of humanity he exemplifies the humanity of science.

Many others have influenced me in significant ways, including Colin
Loftin, Joe Weis, Charles Tittle, Michael Gottfredson, Mark Stafford,
Delbert Elliott, John and Jim Galliher, Robert Sampson, Robert Meier,
Alfred Blumstein, Ronald Akers, Robert Bursik, Dwight Oberholtzer,
and Richard Jobst. I need not elaborate on how these scholars have
affected my thinking and career. They know.

Numerous people contributed to the production of this book.
James Short and Jack Gibbs read and critiqued the entire manuscript,
as did several anonymous reviewers. Mary Child, my editor at
Cambridge University Press, saw value in the work and helped guide
me through the complex process of publication. My production editor,
Russell Hahn, brought his copyediting skills and considerable profes-
sional experience to the task, and series editors Alfred Blumstein and
David Farrington lent their support throughout the project. I am grate-
ful to all of these individuals and to the many fine people at Cambridge
University Press for their assistance.

Finally, to my wife and my sons, who have tolerated me all these
years, I can only offer my affection and love, for which there is no
measure.

CHAPTER ONE

Introduction

On a warm, clear Sunday morning, I walked out onto the deck at the rear of my house to read the morning newspaper. The house sits atop a high, steep hill that looks down upon a nearby street lined with homes on either side. As I sat engrossed in the events of the day, the air was suddenly punctuated by the sound of loud and garrulous voices wending up from below. Glancing down, I saw four young males walking together up the steep slope of the street. Judging from their size and dress, they appeared to be about fourteen or fifteen years of age, though it was difficult to estimate their age with any certainty from the distance at which I was observing.

As they ambled up the street, these young men turned abruptly to one side of the road and climbed up onto the foundation of an expensive new home under construction near the edge of a narrow, precipitous gorge. Trees surrounding the construction site allowed only fleeting glimpses of the boys, but the nature of their activity was evident from the sounds emanating from the site. The crack of splintering wood, the explosive impacts of bricks and other materials being hurled down the hill, the sound of concrete bags tearing open, all testified to the damage these boys were inflicting on the home, damage that probably amounted to many thousands of dollars. A few short minutes later, the boys abruptly quit the scene and disappeared up the street, leaving me once again to myself and the peaceful calm of the morning.

To a sociologist and criminologist, the general features of this event were not remarkable. Indeed, they were almost boringly predictable. The offenders were in the "crime-prone" age group (middle teens to young adulthood); they were males; they were in a group; the event was brief; and, judging from the circumstances, it was not contemplated or planned in advance. In all likelihood, the incident was not reported to the police, nor were the offenders arrested or charged with a criminal offense.

The larger and less easily answered question raised by the event, however, is: Why did it happen? Consider a few of the possibilities. Clearly the *opportunity* for a crime (an attractive and unguarded target) existed, and opportunity is a necessary – though not sufficient – condition for crime. Just as clearly, these boys were not under the supervision of their parents or any other adults at the time the event took place, nor were their moral reservations (if any) about the damage they were inflicting sufficient to prevent the offense.

Aside from such inhibitory factors, however, what about the matter of motivation? What exactly prompted these individuals to engage in such conduct, conduct they surely knew to be illegal? Perhaps they were under the influence of alcohol or some other substance at the time of the event. Given the time of day and their demeanor, however, that seems unlikely. Perhaps they were influenced by the stresses and strains of economic deprivation, or simply felt they had nothing to lose. Yet they were nicely dressed and lived (evidently) in a neighborhood of expensive homes and late-model cars. Maybe the boys suffered from some character disorder or neurophysiological deficit that was present from an early age and of which this event was merely one of many manifestations. Perhaps so, but would one expect *all* of these boys to have that disorder or deficit?

No single event, of course, can establish patterns or causes of behavior. Science is the study not of the unique, after all, but of the general. Nevertheless, even an isolated event can provide tantalizing clues to more general processes. In this instance, the event described here serves to illustrate one of the central issues of this book. Of all the features of this event that might have causal significance, the single most important or determinative feature may have been the simple fact that it was committed by a *group* of individuals acting together. In other words, something about the presence of companions during the event provided the motivation, and perhaps the means, to carry out the crime.

If one were to distill the results of criminological research over the past century, only a few conclusions could be stated with great confidence. As noted earlier, for example, no contemporary criminologist would dispute the contention that criminal behavior is disproportionately committed by the young, or that it is more common among males than among females. The evidence for these phenomena is simply too extensive to be denied (see Chapter 5). Yet there is even stronger evidence for another conclusion: Criminal conduct is predominantly social behavior. Most offenders are imbedded in a network of friends who also break the law, and the single strongest predictor of criminal behavior known to criminologists is the number of delinquent friends an individual has (see Chapters 3 and 4). Furthermore, most delinquent conduct occurs in groups; the group nature of delinquent behavior is one of its most consistently documented features (see Chapter 3).

These facts are known to all criminologists, but for reasons that remain elusive, some fail to appreciate the tenacity of these findings or to recognize their potential implications. Worse yet, some vigorously deny those implications but offer little or no empirical evidence for their position. The general public, for its part, seems to be well aware of the social nature of crime. One of the most powerful signals prompting fear of crime in everyday life is the sight of a *group* of young males (Warr, 1990), and the idea of peer influence as a cause of crime seems to be well entrenched in the folklore of crime. More than half of respondents in one national survey attributed teen violence to "peer pressure" (Maguire and Pastore, 1996).

Confronted with overwhelming evidence of the social character of crime, any honest social scientist would seek answers to certain unavoidable questions: Is the group nature of criminal behavior merely incidental, or does it have etiological significance? If peer influence does operate in criminal events, what exactly is its nature? What does the group nature of crime imply about criminal careers, the prevention of crime, and the plasticity of criminality as a personal trait?

The guiding premise of this book is that the social nature of criminal behavior is not merely an incidental feature of crime, but is instead a potential key to understanding its etiology and some of its most distinctive features. A secondary premise is that the age distribution of criminal behavior and the social nature of crime are not independent or isolated phenomena, but are instead closely connected to one another. It is for that reason that a substantial portion of this book is devoted to understanding the phase of life between childhood and adulthood that we call adolescence. Both of these premises may be incorrect, of course. But if so, it is important to know that they *are* incorrect, for they form the foundation for a good deal of research and theoretical speculation in criminology.

The organization of the book is simple and straightforward. The following chapter reviews the scientific evidence on adolescence and the role of peers during that complex period of life. Chapter 3 discusses the group nature of delinquency and the organization (or lack thereof) of delinquent groups. Chapter 4, the most extensive portion of the book, considers the possible mechanisms by which peer influence may promote or encourage delinquency. Chapter 5 examines the relative influence of two powerful institutions in adolescents' lives – parents and peers – and considers whether peer influence can explain some of the most persistent and controversial features of criminal behavior. The concluding chapter offers a summary and analysis, and suggests some avenues for research on peer influence.

PRELIMINARY ISSUES

Before we can embark on an investigation of peer influence, several antecedent issues must be confronted. The first concerns the meaning of the term "group." When referring to group delinquency, criminologists have traditionally had in mind any delinquent event that involves two or more offenders, or "co-offenders," in Reiss's (1986) terms (see Klein, 1969). That conception surely stipulates an essential element of groups – multiple actors – but some sociologists and social psychologists would insist on additional elements, including an established role structure, shared norms, a shared identity, and common goals (e.g., Theodorson and Theodorson, 1979). As we will see later, however, some of those features are precisely what delinquent groups often lack. Nevertheless, for purposes of historical consistency, and because it is preferable to treat most features of groups as variables rather than as definitional attributes, the former, more liberal definition of a group will be employed throughout this book. Accordingly, the phrase "delinquent group" will be used to refer to any group that includes illegal behavior among its activities, regardless of how frequent or serious that behavior may be, and regardless of how long the group itself persists through time.

Another important issue pertains to the distinction between "groups" and "gangs." The twentieth century produced a rich ethnographic literature on gangs, from Thrasher's (1927) early account of Chicago gangs to more recent descriptions of ethnic gang life in American cities (e.g., Jankowski, 1991). The point at which a group becomes a "gang," however, has been debated for decades in the gang literature (e.g., Miller, 1974; Ball and Curry, 1995; Short, 1997) with no sign of imminent closure. Still, there is general agreement, supported by empirical evidence, that gangs constitute only a small fraction of delinquent groups, and that a ganglike structure is not a prerequisite for delinquent behavior (see especially Morash, 1983; Stafford, 1984). A focus on group as opposed to gang delinquency is therefore eminently defensible, but it is important to emphasize that the discussion of group delinquency throughout this book is not intended to exclude gangs. Gangs are merely institutionalized groups, which is to say that they persist in time as *identifiable* social units, even as their membership changes constantly over the months and years. By all indications, what is true of delinquent groups – unclear and shifting role assignments and role definitions, predominantly same-sex composition, constantly changing membership – is ordinarily true of gangs as well. Even the size of gangs, which seems clearly to differentiate them from most delinquent groups, is misleading, because gangs are often loose aggregations of smaller, age-segregated cliques (see Klein and Crawford, 1967; Sarnecki, 1986). In the end, of course, gangs *are* groups, and the issues to be examined in this book are no less pertinent for gangs than for other groups.

Some other matters require clarification as well. For those who value precision in language, the term "influence" (as in "peer influence") is something of a weasel word, connoting a rather amorphous variety of possible mechanisms of social influence. Nevertheless, that term is used regularly in this book. My defense to the crime is necessity; the actual operative mechanisms of peer influence are not clearly understood, and one of the very purposes of this work is to clarify and narrow the meaning of that phrase.

A few things, however, can be said at this point about the meaning of influence. The idea of peer influence is not unfamiliar to most adults (certainly not to experienced parents), but lay conceptions of peer influence often rest on some vague notion of attitude or value transmission. "Bad" kids influence "good" kids, in other words, by changing their moral standards or other beliefs and attitudes. That is a possibility, to be sure, but everyday experience teaches us that people sometimes conform their behavior to that of others without actually agreeing with them (e.g., children conform to their parents, best friends to one another, employees to their coworkers or boss, and individuals to their leisure, church, sporting, neighborhood, or professional associates). That is why social psychologists often distinguish between *compliance* and *private acceptance*.

> Compliance refers to overt behavior which becomes more like the behavior that the group wishes its members to show. The term refers to outward actions without consideration of the private convictions of the actor. When we speak of "compliance only," we mean that the person is behaving as the group wants him to but does not really believe in what he is doing. That is, he is going along with the group without privately agreeing with the group. (Kiesler and Kiesler, 1970: 3)

Private acceptance, on the other hand,

> means a change in attitude or belief in the direction of group attitudes and beliefs. In this case, the person may not only act as the group wishes, but changes his opinions so that he believes as the group believes. (Kiesler and Kiesler, 1970: 3–4)

There is reason to believe that compliance and private acceptance occur under different circumstances (Kiesler and Kiesler, 1970), but my purpose here is merely to emphasize that, when it comes to delinquent behavior, peer influence does not necessarily entail private acceptance of the behavior by all (or even *any*) members of a group (see Chapter 4). Still, the idea that behavior mirrors attitudes is so intuitively appealing that what is undeniably the most famous theory of peer influence in the history of criminology – Sutherland's (1947) theory of differential association – was built squarely on the idea of private acceptance. However, Sutherland's theory, which predated modern social and behavioral psychology, has faltered in important respects when subjected to empirical test (see Chapter 4).

On a different matter, it is important to differentiate between two concepts that routinely appear in the literature of criminology – "peer influence" and "group delinquency." These concepts refer to overlapping but not necessarily identical phenomena. Most delinquent behavior is committed by groups of adolescents, and some accounts of delinquency stress this fact to explain the onset of delinquent events (see Chapters 3 and 4). However, it is reasonable to suppose that adolescents can be influenced by peers who are not actually present during a delinquent event (including occasions when an offender acts alone), or even by peers whom they have never actually encountered (e.g., teenage celebrities, television actors, role models at school). From time to time, adolescents may also find themselves in groups with persons they do not know at all and whose influence on them, if any, is purely situational and transitory. To complicate matters further, the behavior of adolescents is presumably affected not only by their *current* friends but also by persons they have known in the past.

"Peer influence" and "group delinquency," therefore, are not necessarily analogous concepts. They may entail different etiological processes (see Chapter 4), and adolescents may be affected by persons outside the immediate circle of co-offenders who accompany them on any given occasion. Despite these differences, it appears that, in real life, the sets of associates specified by these two concepts are far from mutually exclusive. Adolescents who engage in delinquency ordinarily do so with their friends (Warr, 1996), and those friends appear to be the same persons with whom they associate when *not* engaged in delinquency. In interviews with two birth cohorts of males living in Racine, Wisconsin, Lyle Shannon (1991) asked these young males whether the persons who had accompanied them during delinquent events were "the people that you usually ran around with." The overwhelming majority of respondents (90 percent for the first reported offense in the Racine sample) answered affirmatively. As for the impact of past associates, the behavior of adolescents at any particular point in time more closely matches that of their *current* friends than that of their prior friends (Warr, 1993a).

This evidence suggests that those persons who are the primary source of delinquent influence upon an adolescent at any given time are the very persons most likely to be present during actual delinquent events, even if one or more may be absent during any particular event. If this is indeed so, then it helps to considerably narrow the range of relevant actors who require attention from investigators and practitioners. Still, it scarcely begins to resolve a host of unanswered questions about peer influence that require attention (see Chapters 3 and 4).

Turning to one final preliminary matter, the terms "crime" and "delinquency" are often used interchangeably in this book to avoid monotony. In a legal sense, of course, the terms are not identical. Delinquent offenses are those committed by minors, whereas criminal offenses are, by definition, committed by adults. However, with the exception of status offenses (acts like smoking and curfew violation that are illegal only for minors), the terms "crime" and "delinquency" refer to the same class of behaviors. Furthermore, because adult offenders ordinarily begin committing crimes as juveniles (Wolfgang, Thornberry, and Figlio, 1987; Shannon, 1988), the terms frequently apply to the same *people*, albeit at different life stages. For these reasons, some criminologists regard the distinction as wholly arbitrary, at least from a behavioral point of view. I share that view; but where age is a relevant consideration in the present discussion, I have tried to make that fact apparent either explicitly or through context.

This initial discussion gives some idea of the conceptual and empirical complexity surrounding the notion of peer influence, and such complexity may be one reason that criminologists have failed to examine the issue as thoroughly as one might expect. Beneath the apparent complexity of the world, however, often lies an elegant simplicity, and it is with that vision in mind that we proceed to examine the role of peers in the lives of adolescents.

CHAPTER TWO

Peers in the Life Course

The term "peer" properly refers to a social equal (Hartup, 1983), but it is conventionally used by social scientists to refer to associates of the same age. In the course of daily living, individuals normally interact with persons from all stages of life, but it is among age-mates that the most intimate of human relationships – deep and abiding friendships and romantic relationships – are often formed.

Sociologists and developmental psychologists are virtually unanimous in agreeing that peer relations play a critical role during the transition from childhood to adulthood, when individuals must cast off their childhood identity and enter the larger world of adults:

> An integral feature of adolescence is the gradual severance of the early emotional ties with parents. . . . At a time when uncertainty and self-doubt is greatest and when support is most needed, many adolescents find themselves in an emotional position where it is difficult, if not impossible, to turn to their parents. Under such circumstances it is hardly surprising that peers play an unusually important role. (Coleman, 1980: 409)

Because peers take on heightened importance during the teenage years, and because criminal behavior peaks at these ages as well, it is natural to wonder whether the two phenomena are somehow linked.

Before we can address that question, however, it is important to look more closely at the role of peers in human development.

PEERS IN THE LIFE COURSE

The concepts of adolescence and peer influence seem to go hand in hand, but there is no necessary reason to assume that peer influence is restricted to adolescence. Most adults, after all, have friends of the same age, as do children. There is general agreement among social scientists, however, that peer influence reaches its zenith between the middle teens and early adulthood. Young children are able to recognize and differentiate age-mates from other persons (e.g., "big boys" or "grown-ups") and will adjust their behavior accordingly, but the lives of young children are dominated by their parents (Hartup, 1983). By the age of about eleven, however, a great deal of children's social activity in the United States occurs with other children, and nearly all persons of this age can identify one or more groups or "cliques" (same-age, same-sex, same-race groups of about three to nine members) to which they belong (Hartup, 1983; Rubin, Bukowski, and Parker, 1998).

By the time they reach their middle teens, it is not uncommon for adolescents to spend more time with their peers than with their parents. In an extraordinarily detailed account of the daily activities of adolescents in a community near Chicago, Csikszentmihalyi and Larson (1984: 67) reported that "teenagers spend one third of their day conversing with others, by far the single most prevalent activity in their lives... Three times as much of it occurs with friends as with parents or other adults; 13 percent occurs by phone." What is more, "a full half of the week's waking hours are spent with peers – partly in the classroom and partly with friends outside of class" (1984: 71). Summing up their investigation, Csikszentmihalyi and Larson concluded that "in terms of sheer amount of time, peers are by far the greatest presence in an adolescent's life" (1984: 71). Ironically, the major competitor for adolescents' time is not interaction with adults (including parents) but *solitude,* which occupies about one-fourth of the day on average.

Not only do peers dominate daily social interaction, but Csikszentmihalyi and Larson's analysis of mood variations throughout the day
showed that it is in the company of peers that adolescents "feel most
happy, alert, and intrinsically motivated" (1984: 75).

> When teenagers socialize with friends, they talk about differ-
> ent things than when they socialize with family members. With
> friends, talk is typically joking and buoyant; it deals with topics
> such as sports, relationships, gossip, and general goofing around.
> With family, particularly during the relatively few talks with par-
> ents, the interaction is more serious and topics include college,
> work around the house, the state of the world, and the family
> vacation. Nonetheless, talking with family is nearly as positive as
> with friends. (1984: 102)

In addition to Csikszentmihalyi and Larson's research, national
longitudinal self-report data from young people indicate that time
spent with peers increases dramatically during adolescence (see Warr,
1993a). By itself, however, time spent with peers is not necessarily an accurate indicator of peer influence, if only because some of that shared
time is compulsory. Setting aside time per se, one of the best-known
analyses of peer influence during adolescence comes from Berndt
(1979), who surveyed schoolchildren in grades three, six, nine, and
eleven or twelve and asked the children how they would respond in
situations where their friends encouraged them to engage in illegal
or immoral conduct of which they, themselves, disapproved. Berndt's
investigation revealed that "conformity to peers on antisocial behavior
increased greatly between third and ninth grades, and then declined"
(1979: 615). In a similar study reported in the same article, Berndt
found that even as conformity to peers rises and falls from grades
three through twelve, conformity to *parents* exhibits an uninterrupted
decline during the same period. The decline is fairly modest in size,
however, and does not match the extraordinary change in peer conformity that takes place at this stage of life.

Warr (1993a) uncovered similar evidence of a curvilinear age
distribution of peer influence in responses to survey questions from
the National Youth Survey (e.g., "If your friends got into trouble with

the police, would you be willing to lie to protect them?"), and both
he and Berndt commented on the strong similarity between the age
distribution of peer influence and delinquent behavior itself (see also
Steinberg and Silverberg, 1986; Fuligni and Eccles, 1993). Indeed,
Warr found that when exposure to delinquent peers was held constant,
the association between age and delinquency disappeared for most of
the offenses that he examined. Still other studies that have relied on
Asch-type measures of peer conformity agree that "the suggestibility
of the child to peer influence increases with age into pubescence after
which the efficacy of peer influence in inducing public conformity
declines with increasing age" (Costanzo, 1980: 206).

CROSS-CULTURAL VARIATION IN PEER INTERACTION

One of the most telling questions that can be asked about peer interaction in adolescence is whether its features vary from one culture to the next, or from one historical era to another. If there is
some substantial degree of uniformity and universality to peer associations, then it is easier to argue that peer interaction is a natural
or normal part of the human developmental process. On the other
hand, such similarity would make it more difficult to ascribe cross-
national or temporal variation in crime rates to differences in peer
relations.

The evidence on this matter is refreshingly clear, if not always as
current as one would wish. Peer interaction in everyday life varies considerably from culture to culture, as well as historically. In some societies, parents actively discourage and constrain associations between
their children and age-mates, placing a firm choke hold on any influences outside the family. In other societies, peer interaction is not only
tolerated but encouraged as an essential ingredient of normal social
development.

An example of the former seems to be the French, who attempt to
keep their children oriented toward their parents and family rather
than toward their peers. Mussen, Conger, and Kagan (1979: 388) observe that

French parents, who traditionally teach their children to remain close to the family group, do not encourage play with other children. In general, European children are much less likely than Americans to rely on peers, rather than on adults, for opinions and advice.

Devereux (1970) reported that German parents relinquish little control over their children until late adolescence, resulting in a "postponement of... participation in semiautonomous peer group activity" (1970: 101). When Devereux and his associates compared American and German adolescents, they were "struck by the apparently much greater social maturity and sophistication of American youngsters in their middle teens" (1970: 101). However, they also noted that American youngsters seem to have greater problems with self-control and autonomy later in life.

The extremes between cultures with respect to peer practices are well illustrated by Csikszentmihalyi and Larson (1984), who compared self-reports from American adolescents with published data from the Soviet Union and Japan:

> In the Soviet Union and Japan, teenagers reported spending two to three hours per week with friends; for our sample, this figure was approximately twenty hours. Among modern societies, American youth have a special freedom to enjoy time among themselves. (1984: 173)

Indeed, a ratio of 8:1 in peer time from one culture to another, if true, is nothing short of startling.

One of the most careful and thorough cross-cultural studies of peer interaction comes from Kandel and Lesser (1972), who compared adolescents in the United States and Denmark. Danish youngsters, they found, have fewer friends (often only one at a time) than their American counterparts, but their friendships are deeper. Danish adolescents commonly view their parents as companions, whereas American adolescents usually turn to their peers for companionship and are more likely to prefer the company of their peers to that of their parents. Adolescents in both countries rely on their parents and friends for advice, but in different ways. Danish adolescents, for example, are much more likely to go to friends with moral questions (Americans go to their parents or other adults), but rely more heavily on their parents for advice about career plans, school grades, or college.

Another cross-cultural study calls into question the common assumption that the norms and values of adolescents are intrinsically antithetical to those of adults. Unlike their American counterparts, it seems, Soviet children expect their peers to *endorse* adult standards:

> Growing up in an atmosphere of adult-peer cross pressure is apparently part of the standard experience for the American child. In contrast, the Soviet child in this study – and also in another done more recently – apparently perceive their peer group as carrying essentially the same norms as those of their parents and teachers. (Devereux, 1970: 126; see also Bronfenbrenner, 1967)

HISTORICAL AND STRUCTURAL VARIATION

Variation in peer relations can be examined over time as well as cross-culturally. The historian John Gillis (1974), who disputes Aries's (1962) well-known contention that adulthood followed immediately upon childhood in preindustrial Europe, has argued that child mortality rates were so high in England and Europe in the centuries leading up to the industrial revolution that couples often produced many children in hopes that some might survive to adulthood to maintain the family name and property. In families where multiple children survived, younger children were often viewed as superfluous and left home as early as age eight or nine. Some of these "surplus" children were absorbed into other households as servants; others became apprentices, students, or novitiates in the church, or were handed off through the custom of "claiming kin" (sending youngsters to live with relatives). But large numbers of young people were left to fend for themselves and joined with others their age to form the sorts of communal youth groups (e.g., wandering workers, vagabonds) that flourished at the time and exemplified the popular principle of *fraternité*.

Social Structure

Peer relations can also be examined from the broad vantage point of human societal development. Hunting and gathering societies – the primary form of social organization for most of human existence – were so small (rarely larger than about forty people), and contact among them so infrequent, that exposure to age peers was probably quite limited and primarily restricted to kin. Later forms of preindustrial society – pastoral, horticultural, agrarian – supported larger populations with concomitantly greater opportunities for peer interaction, but size alone seems to be no guarantee of extensive peer interaction or the development of adolescent culture. Some of the largest societies in the modern world – China, Mexico – direct children toward their families rather than toward their peers (Campbell, 1964). In preindustrial societies, the labor of adolescents is often required by the family for farming, herding, milking, planting, and other subsistence tasks, leaving little free time for peers (Schlegel and Barry, 1991).

Anthropologists, to be sure, have documented societies where adolescents spend much or all of their time with one another in age-segregated groups that share living quarters.

> Up to about age 10 or 11, Nyakyusa boys live in their fathers' homes and tend their cattle. When a number of village sons have reached the right age, they are given a piece of land adjacent to the village, where they build their own huts. Along with change of residence goes an occupational change: they leave herding to the younger boys, and work in the fields with their fathers. Thus, they belong to two villages – economically to that of their fathers, and socially to that of their age-mates. While each boy's village is attached to the adult village that gave it land, boys from other villages may live there as well. Until they marry, boys and young men eat at their mothers' hearths, going from one to another in small groups. Beginning with perhaps a dozen boys, new members are added for about six or eight years, and then the village is closed. At about age 25, the senior members begin to marry and cultivate their own fields. The rationale for sending boys away is so that the parents may have privacy in their sexual activities. (Schlegel and Barry, 1991: 69–70, summarizing Wilson, 1963)

In an anthropological survey of preindustrial societies, Schlegel and Barry (1991: 70) report that extensive peer interaction in such societies is not extremely rare:

> It is not uncommon in many societies for adolescent boys to sleep away from their parents' homes. If the community contains a men's house, it is the usual sleeping place for adolescent boys, unmarried – widowed or divorced – men, and men who for various reasons are sleeping apart from their wives. For example, Hopi boys after about age 10 or 11 frequently sleep in the kivas, the ceremonial buildings used as men's houses, or on warm nights, in groups on the flat rooftops of the family houses.

Still, the authors note that peers are primary agents of socialization in a relatively small percentage of cultures (for boys, only 11 of the 176 societies examined), and they state that "[i]n most societies, adolescents spend most of their time in a family, usually their own. In the majority of societies, then, some accommodation must be made between attachment to family and attachment to peers" (1991: 71). As a general rule in preindustrial societies, say Schlegel and Barry, "peer groups are not the enemies of parents" (1991: 74). Peer groups often share the norms of the larger culture, and may even have the primary responsibility to enforce those norms as part of the rearing of children and the punishing of deviants.

Industrial Societies

At the extreme end of the developmental continuum are the rigidly age-graded structures of modern advanced industrial societies. In such societies, an extended period of mandatory education postpones entry into adulthood well beyond physical maturity, encourages age-segregated interaction through age-graded classrooms, and creates a distinct phase of life ("adolescence") that helps support a youth subculture (Erikson, 1960; J. S. Coleman, 1974; Greenberg, 1985; Moffitt, 1993; Felson, 1994). Although the educational system in industrial societies is a chief source of age segregation, the idea of age-segregated education itself appears to be a recent historical development. As late as the eighteenth century, students in many European countries attended school with classmates of widely varying ages (even young adults), a practice that persisted in rural America into the twentieth century (Aries, 1962; J. S. Coleman, 1974).

James Coleman (1974) has documented the astonishing transformation in the lives of the young that took place in the United States as it grew from an agricultural into an industrial society. In the rural, agrarian America of the nineteenth century, children worked alongside adults from an early age; school was seasonal (if attended at all) and subordinate to work; and age heterogeneity characterized the family (including siblings), schoolmates, and even youth groups, in which older adolescents and young adults shared their leisure hours with those as young as twelve or thirteen. As recently as 1900, only a small fraction of American youth graduated from high school; but by the second half of the twentieth century the opposite was true, and a variety of factors – declining seasonal labor, increasing occupational specialization and population concentration, immigration, child labor and compulsory education laws – had combined to produce the standardized, age-graded educational system of today.

Commenting on these changes, Coleman (1974: 2, 9) writes:

> If the success of revolutions is measured entirely by their completeness, certainly the social revolution which has transformed the role of young people in society during the last century has been among the most successful. . . . The world of the maturing child, formerly dominated by the home, is now monopolized on the formal level by the school and on the informal level by the age group. [The family] is a minor part of the social environment of many youth beyond early adolescence.

Industrial societies are structurally conducive to peer interaction, but even among industrial societies, the nature of peer interaction seems to reflect cultural traditions as much as social structure. As we saw earlier, both France and Germany restrict peer interaction outside the school, as does Japan. In the United States, however, the changes in youth wrought by industrialization took place in a society in which the young already enjoyed a good deal of "freedom from direct adult

supervision" in their daily lives (Coleman, 1974: 12). This social feature of the United States evidently stemmed from its cultural blood-
line to England, a country wherein, unlike its European neighbors,
unsupervised play among the young was normative and encouraged
(Youniss, 1980).

CHANGING PEER RELATIONS

Industrialization transformed the lives of the young in the United
States, but the transformation did not cease there. There is reason
to believe that the United States has undergone a significant cultural
shift in recent decades, a shift in which traditional parental authority
and control over socialization has been further ceded to peers. Felson
and Gottfredson (1984; see also Felson, 1994) surveyed a sample of
the Illinois population, asking detailed questions about respondents'
routine activities when they were seventeen years old. By comparing
responses from persons of different generations, these investigators
documented startling declines in the proportion of young persons
who eat dinner at home with the family, who can be found at home or
with an adult after school, who spend Saturday night at home, or who
have household chores in the afternoon.

> Responses indicated dramatic changes in activity patterns over
> the generations, with much more parental control over the older
> generations of teenagers, especially females. To begin, bedtimes
> of 11 p.m. or later were reported among only 17 percent of males
> and 9 percent of females who had turned 18 in 1940 or before.
> In comparison, for those who turned 18 in the 1971 to 1979
> period, approximately half of both sexes reported going to bed
> routinely at 11 p.m. or later.
>
> Respondents who were 17 years old at some point in the 1971
> to 1979 period were more than twice as likely to be away from
> parents on Saturdays as those who were 17 in 1940 or before
> (59 vs. 26 percent for males, respectively; 41 vs. 16 percent for
> females). We also observed an increase in the bewitching hour
> (the time they were expected to be home on Saturday night) from

a median of 11:36 p.m. for males in the oldest group to 1 a.m. for males in the newest group. For females, the corresponding change was from 10:44 p.m. to 12:24 a.m. . . . In the oldest group, only 13 percent of females would be out past 11 p.m. on the average Friday or Saturday night. For the newest group, this increases to 83 percent, more than five times what it had been. In another question . . . respondents indicated that they went out more nights, both during the week and on weekends.

For both males and females, approximately half of the more recent respondents had no afternoon chores, a major increase in "freedom" over the older group. There were also increases in the numbers away in the afternoon; when young people are home in the afternoon, adults are increasingly absent. . . . Perhaps the most interesting finding is that the family dinner together, nearly universal in the older group, declined noticeably for the younger group. (Felson, 1994: 101–3)

Assuming such trends to be real, what is behind them? Felson and Gottfredson (see also Felson, 1994) see much of the reason in the increasing availability and romanticization of the automobile in the United States after the Second World War. The automobile (particularly when American families came to own more than one) provided a means for young people to get away from home and to contact friends who lived some distance away. It became in effect a portable, socially sanctioned meeting place for peer interaction, one whose usefulness for romantic trysts, getting high, listening to music, or just tooling about is still celebrated in popular culture today. Thornburg (1982: 198) seems to be correct in asserting that, among adolescents, the automobile remains "a representation of independence, power, mobility, status, and conquest. It is the single greatest symbol [of status] . . . throughout the high school years."

Another factor underlying the shift has been the increasing tendency of young people to acquire jobs outside the home during high school and college. Not only does work cut into time spent with the family, but the type of work available to young people (often service jobs in places like fast-food restaurants) frequently increases exposure to peers in work environments that are largely unsupervised by adults. Although employment for teenagers is viewed by many as a healthy, worthwhile activity as well as a cure or preventative for delinquent behavior, the ironic truth is that young people who work are more likely to become involved with alcohol or marijuana than those who do not (Ploeger, 1997).

Other social changes seem to have contributed to the peer orientation of American youth, including the increasing proportion of mothers in the workforce, the diminishing number of adults in American households, and the rise of youth culture that was abetted by the baby boom and by the growing affluence of American youth (J. S. Coleman, 1974; Coleman and Hoffer, 1987; Short, 1997). By almost any standard, the lives of the young in the United States today are dominated by peers and peer culture. This fact is evident in the amount of time that young people spend in each others' company, the variety of entertainment, apparel, food and beverage, and other commercial products aimed specifically at adolescents, and by the apparent strength of peer influence in many (though not all) adolescents' lives in the United States (e.g., Csikszentmihalyi and Larson, 1984; Coleman and Hoffer, 1987; Coleman, 1990; Felson, 1994).

PEERS AS AGENTS OF SOCIALIZATION

As we have seen, the quantity and quality of peer interaction varies greatly among countries of the world. Yet it remains true that "none of the world's cultures rears its children solely through interaction with adults" (Hartup, 1983: 104). Some attraction to peers is to be expected among adolescents, if only because "parent-child relationships are inherently asymmetrical [whereas] peer relationships, in contrast, can be more symmetrical and egalitarian" (Fuligni and Eccles, 1993: 623).

As agents of socialization, peers are often thought to be a wholly negative source of influence in adolescents' lives, and it is undeniable that they can in fact play a negative role. Indeed, one commentator insists that "the peer group is not only an unsuitable source for development toward adult goals, it also attenuates the invaluable lines

of communication and culture transmission across the generations"
(J. S. Coleman, 1974:2). Intergenerational *social capital* – the contribution that adults make to the development of the young – is dissi-
pated, he argues, when young people (or, for that matter, adults) are
preoccupied with their own generation (Coleman and Hoffer, 1987;
Coleman, 1990).

Still, many developmental psychologists argue that peer interaction
is an important, even essential element in the successful transition
from childhood to adulthood. What are the benefits of peer interaction? According to a variety of developmental psychologists (e.g.,
Ausubel, 1954; Adams, 1973; Grusec and Lytton, 1988), there are
many. First, peer groups provide the setting in which adolescents establish their first identity outside of the family and begin the process
of emancipation from parents and home.

> As adolescents strive to relinquish psychological dependence
> on parents, peer groups become a temporary replacement until
> fully autonomous (psychological) functioning is possible. Some
> regard the central psychological task of early adolescence to be
> locating a peer group that is not only accepting and supportive
> but also compatible with one's dispositions and interests. It is
> sensible, then, to expect cliques to become more salient and
> also more distant from parents in adolescence, as they take
> on the role of substitute source of psychological dependence.
> (Brown, 1990: 180)

> In the process of loosening emotional ties to the family of ori-
> gin, the adolescent is vulnerable, since he does not yet have a
> sufficiently developed identity or autonomy of his own. To fill
> the void, a new dependency frequently emerges, a dependency
> on his peer group. (Muuss, 1980: 175)

In many ways, peers become a substitute family during adolescence,
providing an independent source of self-esteem, identity, and even
protection.

Peers also provide emotional support during a period of life in
which rapid, almost frenetic changes are occurring – the onset of puberty and physical maturation, constant exposure to new persons at

school, the transition to junior high and high school, new responsibilities related to work and driving an automobile, and, for many, increasing academic demands at school. Families, of course, can and often do provide emotional sustenance through this period as well, but they cannot fully replace the companionship and support that comes from coparticipants in this phase of life, and tensions at home sometimes nullify or offset any support that the family might otherwise afford.

Peer groups are also the context in which one of the most important transitions in life often occurs – the transition from same-sex friendships to opposite-sex friendships and, ultimately, to stable romantic relationships (e.g., Dunphy, 1980; Crockett, Losoff, and Petersen, 1984). Peer groups in late childhood and early adolescence are almost exclusively same-sex groups. Dating is rare and often awkward because of the greater height and maturity of females at this age. By middle adolescence, however, contact with members of the opposite sex increases substantially, though individuals ordinarily retain their membership in unisexual groups. In time, peer groups become increasingly mixed-sexed in composition (though same-sex groups do not disappear), and by late adolescence dating has become normative and there is a great deal of interaction within and between mixed-sex cliques. Eventually, as individuals graduate from high school, existing peer networks begin to dissolve as members enter the work force, go to college, or take other adult paths, and many couples move toward going steady, engagement, or marriage.

Aside from the transition to opposite-sex relationships, adolescent peer groups also appear to be important for the development of social competence and the ability to empathize and share intimacy:

> Through self-disclosure, and by allowing oneself to become vulnerable to a coequal, adolescent friends share with one another their most personal thoughts and feelings, become sensitive to the needs and desires of others, and, in the process, acquire a deep understanding of the other and the self. (Savin-Williams and Berndt, 1990: 278)

> The peer group not only provides social, emotional, and psychological support in the emancipation process, but it teaches basic

social and physical skills that are often not taught at home or in the school. (Muuss, 1980: 175)

By observing and interacting with their peers, adolescents acquire interactional skills and learn the "rules" about work, dating, sex, interpersonal conflict, and life in general.

Investigators have noted still other ways in which peers contribute to development – creating, for example, a sense of membership in a generation and encouraging prosocial behavior (see Mussen, Conger, and Kagan, 1979). However, it is easy to forget the sheer pleasure and fun that friends provide for young people, something that parents in the United States often seem to appreciate and encourage, if sometimes reluctantly.

> Adolescents typically report that they enjoy their activities with friends more than any other. With friends, they feel that they are understood and can fully be themselves. Friends spend much time together simply talking about themselves, other adolescents, or events in the wider world. They relax, joke, watch television or videos, and participate in sports. These moments of enjoyment and companionship contribute to a generational sense of belonging with others who are respected and liked. (Savin-Williams and Berndt, 1990: 279)

When one investigator asked college students what gave their lives meaning, relations with friends was cited more often than any other factor, including family, religion, work, and education (Klinger, 1977).

All of the foregoing points to the conclusion that relations with peers have beneficial as well as detrimental consequences for adolescents. It is tempting (and, for many, irresistible) to reach for a general conclusion as to whether peer influence is ultimately a positive or negative force in the lives of adolescents. The truth is that the question cannot be settled within the current state of research, and may always remain unanswerable. The myriad countervailing effects of peer influence are difficult to quantify and compare, and just as the family may be a positive agency of socialization for some individuals but not for others, so it is with peers. Perhaps the best summary that can now be offered comes from Savin-Williams and Berndt (1990: 306–7):

> Issues of the relative positive and negative merits of peer influ-
> ence and the nature of supportive peer relations remain to be
> resolved. Conforming to peers may restrict individuality, freedom
> of expression, personal development, and future aspirations.
> Having no friends may be preferable to having "bad" friends.
> An adolescent may learn negative behaviors to keep friends, or
> be so concerned with initiating or maintaining friendships that
> she or he feels rejected, jealous, or isolated. We believe, how-
> ever, that the evidence supports the notion that the ideal is a few
> close, intimate friendships that are secure, stable, and recipro-
> cated. . . . Forming successful peer relations is a critical aspect of
> healthy development.

PEER GROUP FORMATION

If peers are central to the lives of adolescents, how exactly are peer
groups formed? What brings adolescents together into friendships,
cliques, and other groups?

Like most human relationships, a critical factor seems to be the
simple but powerful fact of propinquity. Many years ago, Festinger,
Schachter, and Back (1950) demonstrated that residents of a married-
student housing project were most likely to name as their friends those
persons who lived closest to them. With increasing distance, the density
of friendships decreased precipitously. In one of their classic works,
Sherif and Sherif (1964) reported that boys starting summer camp
quickly formed friendships with others who shared the same living
quarters. However, when the boys were reassigned to new housing
units, new friendship patterns readily emerged to replace the old ones.

The remarkable power of propinquity is aptly described by Cairns
and Cairns (1994: 108):

> Human infants tend to become strongly attached with who-
> ever they interact, whether male or female, young or old.
> Caretaking facilitates the attachment, but it is not necessary.
> Propinquity is the necessary factor. Paradoxically, mammalian

infants – monkeys, puppies, lambs – become attached emotionally even to individuals who are punitive if they are kept in close
proximity to them. By controlling propinquity, it is possible not
only to create the conditions for affection and friendship, but
also to manufacture it in the hospital, nursery, and preschool.

The effects of propinquity are not limited to infancy in humans and animals. Beyond childhood, close relationships tend
to become established when people are brought into proximity
to each other, whether the constraints are by employment, training, or geography. Friendships and groups are formed by people
who attend the same college, become assigned to the same military installation, attend the same church, or work together in
the same factory.

For young people, residential proximity is an obvious source of
propinquity, though its effect is no doubt muted in the modern world
(at least among older adolescents) by the automobile. So, too, is the
school. In a longitudinal study of friendship formation, Cairns and
Cairns (1994: 108) discovered that the single best predictor of friendship nominations at any given point in time was the classroom assignments of their subjects.

It might be expected that school-age friendships and groups
are formed by children and adolescents primarily among the
pool of people assigned to the classroom. The facts bear out the
expectation. Regardless of how we sought information about
group affiliations, there was a strong tendency for friendships
and groups to be forged among the relationships available in
the classroom. When classrooms were reshuffled, so were the
friendships and groups.

As powerful as propinquity has proven to be, no less important
in the process of friendship formation is the principle of homophily
(i.e., people befriend people like themselves). In accordance with a
long history of social scientific research, the Cairns (1994) reported
that adolescent friendships were most likely to form among persons
with similar ascriptive characteristics – age, sex (particularly among
younger adolescents), race, and social class – and they also found some
evidence of clustering according to characteristics like popularity,

aggression, achievement, physical maturation, sports participation, physical attractiveness, and leadership.

> Groups tend to form along any salient characteristic where similarity can be defined. This holds for sex, age, race, smoking, failing a grade, aggression, doing well in class, playing football, or being a cheerleader. Once clustered, contagious reciprocity in behaviors and actions appears, creating new types of similarities among cluster members. (1994: 114)

Although classroom assignments resulted in frequent changes in friends, the Cairns found that students tended to find their friends from among a larger, identifiable pool of individuals who resembled themselves.

Taken together, homophily and propinquity are powerful predictors of friendship formation, and they carry over to delinquent associations as well (e.g., Reiss and Farrington, 1991). As we will see later, these phenomena have important implications for understanding the role of peer influence in delinquent behavior.

PARENTS VERSUS PEERS

Among the most frequently raised questions surrounding adolescence is the relative strength of parental and peer influence during this period of life. Some studies claim that peer influence generally exceeds that of parents during adolescence (see Thornburg, 1982). For example, in one famous investigation, Coleman (1961) found that a larger percentage of high school students said that they would be unhappy if their "best friend did not like what they did" than if their parents or teachers did not like what they did. Other studies, however, claim to show that parental influence generally outweighs that of peers (see Larson, 1980; Thornburg, 1982).

Many investigators view the question of "parents versus peers" as simplistic, because one source of influence may dominate in one domain of life but not in another. An early and influential test of this so-called situation hypothesis was conducted by Brittain (e.g., 1963), who provided evidence that adolescents turn to peers for help with current dilemmas and to parents for help with future concerns (e.g., educational/employment plans). In a similar way, others have argued that peer influence is dominant in such areas as leisure behavior, "youth-related" behaviors, and interpersonal relationships (see Kandel and Lesser, 1972; Kandel, 1974; Thornburg, 1982; Meeus, 1989).

In one of the more incisive investigations of the situation hypothesis, Larson (1980) found that some adolescents tended to be either peer-compliant or parent-compliant when faced with hypothetical dilemmas (for example, whether or not to turn in a friend to the principal, or to go to a prohibited party), but many made decisions based on the content of the situation rather than on the wishes of parents *or* peers. Larson did not deny the strength of parental or peer influence, but argued that it is determinative only for a minority of adolescents, and only in some situations. And he questioned whether the conventional means of measuring such influence (i.e., responses to hypothetical situations where parents or peers approve or disapprove of certain actions) can adequately capture that influence.

What discussions of parental and peer influence so often overlook is that these two sources of influence *interact* with one another. Research suggests that highly peer-oriented children often have parents who are either permissive (especially when it comes to monitoring their children's activities) or who do not relax their power and restrictiveness as their children grow and gain autonomy (Fuligni and Eccles, 1993). Striking a proper balance between these two poles is admittedly difficult, but it is evidently crucial, for parenting styles not only affect the general peer orientation of children but the probability that they will acquire delinquent friends as well (see Chapter 5).

The relative influence of parents and peers remains an unsettled question today, but what can be said with confidence is that, for most adolescents, parental influence is quite strong in some domains, particularly in the area of long-term goals such as educational and occupational aspirations (Kandel and Lesser, 1969, 1972; Thornburg, 1982). In other areas, however, peers seem to dominate, and their influence in one domain – delinquent behavior – is a matter to which we will be turning shortly.

CHAPTER THREE

The Group Character of Crime and Delinquency

The preceding chapter demonstrated the importance of peers in the lives of most adolescents, and the next chapter will examine how peer influence can exert itself when it comes to delinquent conduct. Before considering the nature of peer influence, however, it is important to understand the nature of delinquent behavior itself. Are most delinquent acts the work of solitary offenders who operate without the co-operation or support of others, or are they acts committed by groups of adolescents? If the latter, are these groups large or small, stable or unstable, homogeneous or heterogeneous, organized or disorganized? Without some understanding of the nature of delinquent events, it is premature to speculate on their causes.

DELINQUENCY AS GROUP BEHAVIOR

One of the most consistently reported features of delinquent behavior is its group nature. Throughout the last century, investigators have noted a tendency for offenders to commit delinquent acts in the company of others. The "gregarious and companionate character" of delinquency, as Empey (1982: 121) has described it, was documented more than seventy years ago by Shaw and McKay (1931), who discovered that more than 80 percent of juveniles appearing before the Chicago

Juvenile Court had accomplices. Similar findings drawn from official data were regularly reported by scholars from the 1920s through the 1960s (see Klein, 1969; Erickson, 1971; Reiss, 1986).

As self-report methodology came to be widely adopted by criminologists, evidence for the group nature of delinquency mounted. For example, Gold (1970) reported that 75 percent of the 2,490 chargeable delinquent offenses reported by his sample of Flint youth were committed in the company of others, and less than 20 percent of respondents in Shannon's (1991: 23) survey of Racine youth "said that they had done what they did while alone." Erickson (1971), Erickson and Jensen (1977), and Warr (1996) uncovered consistently high "group violation rates" (the proportion of offenses committed in groups) in self-report data from juveniles. Only one of the eighteen offenses examined by Erickson had a group violation rate below 50 percent, and the same was true of only four of eighteen offenses in Erickson and Jensen's (1977) study, and only two of twelve in Warr's (1996). Furthermore, some of the exceptions to the rule were acts that had some inherently solitary element to them (e.g., defying parents, running away; see Erickson and Jensen, 1977).

Evidence for the group nature of delinquency also comes from countries outside the United States (Sarnecki, 1986; Reiss and Farrington, 1991). Sarnecki's (1986) account of the social connections among delinquents in a southern Swedish city suggests that delinquency is virtually incomprehensible without attention to its social character.

Even though delinquency is predominantly group behavior, it remains true that some offenses are more likely to be committed in groups than others. Disparities in the definitions and kinds of offenses measured in self-report studies make it difficult to reach firm conclusions on the matter, but a few generalizations are defensible. There is consistent evidence that alcohol and marijuana are used by adolescents almost exclusively in group settings. Likewise, certain property and public order offenses (vandalism, burglary, trespassing) have rates of group offending nearly as high as those for drug offenses, with other property crimes (e.g., auto theft) not far behind. On the other side of the scale, shoplifting and assault (or threatening assault) appear to be among the less "groupy" offenses, a matter to which we shall return (see Gold, 1970; Erickson, 1971; Erickson and Jensen, 1977; Reiss and Farrington, 1991; Warr, 1996).

Some skeptics point to offenses with low group violation rates, like assault, as evidence that the group nature of delinquency is overstated. But offense-specific group violation rates can have little bearing on the *total* group violation rate, because some offenses are committed much more frequently than others. Gold found that the offenses most frequently committed by juveniles were the ones most often committed in groups, from which he surmised that "youngsters more often commit those kinds of offenses which others will commit with them" (1970: 83; see also Hindelang, 1976; Reiss, 1986).

Information about group delinquency comes primarily from self-report and official data, and those data typically pertain to events or incidents of crime. Reiss (1986), however, has noted that data on the group composition of *events* cannot be used to estimate the group participation rate of *offenders*, which is ordinarily higher. To illustrate, he shows that about one-half of all burglaries committed by juveniles in one city during an eight-year period were committed by groups. But the one-half of *incidents* committed by those groups involved two-thirds of all *offenders*. By their very nature, event- or incident-based data tend to understate group involvement, because they give equal weight to lone and group offenses. The same issue applies to victims as well as offenders, which is why victimization surveys like the National Crime Victimization Survey distinguish between *incidents* and *victimizations* (O'Brien, 1995).

In what may be the most comprehensive review of research on group delinquency ever undertaken, Reiss (1986: 145, 152) concluded that "group offending is most characteristic of what we think of as juvenile delinquency, and characterizes juvenile careers. . . . Solo offending is relatively uncommon at young ages and does not become the modal form of offending until the late teens or early twenties." These statements succinctly summarize the evidence on group delinquency, and it is important to note that the transition to lone offending mentioned by Reiss takes place at the very time that most offenders are leaving crime behind. Adolescents ordinarily desist from crime by the time they reach their twenties (see Chapter 5), and although the minority who persist appear to be predominantly lone offenders, it remains unclear whether they were *always* so. Research by Reiss and Farrington (1991: 393), however, suggests that diminished rates of co-offending among older offenders occur "primarily because individual offenders change and become less likely to offend with others," and not because of the "persistence of those who offend . . . alone."

FEATURES OF DELINQUENT GROUPS

If delinquency is primarily a group phenomenon, what are the distinguishing features of delinquent groups? To answer that question, let us begin with one of the earliest investigations of the subject.

Among the first to conduct empirical research on delinquent groups were Shaw and McKay, whose 1931 *Report on the Causes of Crime* contained a lucid section on "The Companionship Factor in Juvenile Delinquency." Shaw and McKay analyzed data from the Juvenile Court of Cook County for the year 1928. Their best-known discovery, noted earlier, was that approximately four-fifths (81.8 percent) of the offenses coming before the court involved two or more offenders. Although they described other quantitative properties of group offending as well, the bulk of Shaw and McKay's analysis was given over to an extended description of a single delinquent – Sidney Blotzman – whose career, they argued, possessed "certain aspects that are common to a statistically high proportion of the cases of male juvenile delinquents appearing in the juvenile court of Chicago" (1931: 200).

Sidney grew up in a highly "deteriorated" neighborhood west of the Loop in a family marked by frequent desertion of the father. He moved with his family to a nearby neighborhood when he was ten and moved yet again when he was fifteen. Sidney was first arrested in 1916 at about age eight for petty theft, and last arrested in 1925 at age sixteen for armed robbery and rape. All but two of the thirteen offenses for which he was arrested were committed with accomplices. Over the course of his delinquent career, Sidney was affiliated with three delinquent groups, each of which inhabited the neighborhood in which he resided at the time. Although these groups were fairly large, and although Sidney was arrested with a total of eleven different co-offenders over the course of his career, he *never* committed an offense with more than three companions on any one occasion. In his first group, which contained six members, Sidney committed offenses with four distinct subsets (triads) of the group. The two groups to which he later belonged were considerably larger (more than a dozen), but in both cases Sidney committed offenses with only a small portion of the group (three members), usually with no more than two of them at any one time.

Shaw and McKay emphasized the fact that the larger groups with which Sidney was affiliated existed before he joined them, that each had its own unique repertoire of offenses, and that Sidney's own history of offending closely paralleled the activities of the groups to which he belonged: "The successive types of delinquent activity in which Sidney engaged, beginning with pilfering in the neighborhood and progressing to larceny of automobiles and robbery with a gun, show a close correspondence with the delinquent patterns prevailing in the successive groups with which he had contact" (1931: 221).

Shaw and McKay also pointed to the importance of age relations in delinquent groups. Sidney committed his first delinquent act with an older boy (Joseph Kratz) from his neighborhood, a boy who had a history of delinquency and who, in Sidney's own words, "knew so much about life and I liked him, and so I made him my idol" (1931: 223). The authors also noted of Sidney that "all but two of his delinquencies and crimes took place while he was in the company of older offenders" (1931: 204), and they further observed how the "specialized pattern of delinquency" in each of Sidney's groups was "handed down from the older to the younger members of the group" (1931: 213).

The third and last group with which Sidney was affiliated consisted of younger members of an adult criminal group, a group which, according to Shaw and McKay, "included some of Chicago's most notorious criminals" (1931: 218). It was with members of this group that Sidney committed his most serious offenses, including the armed robbery and rape for which he ultimately received a twenty-year prison sentence.

Other Features of Delinquent Groups

Since the time of Shaw and McKay's work, most research on delinquent groups has consisted of scattered small-scale studies employing nonprobability samples, and many contemporary assumptions about delinquent groups rest on only a single study or source of data (see Reiss, 1986). Still, some of the elements of Sidney's biography can be seen in this literature.

The most solidly established feature of offending groups is their size; nearly all studies show typical group sizes in the range of two to four members (Shaw and McKay, 1931; Gold, 1970; Hood and Sparks, 1970; Reiss, 1986; Sarnecki, 1986; Warr, 1996). It appears, furthermore, that group size diminishes with age; groups of four or more are not uncommon in late childhood and early adolescence, but gradually give way to triads and dyads in middle and late adolescence (Hood and Sparks, 1970; Reiss, 1986). Lone offending is most typical of adult offenders, presumably because, compared to the young, they are less apt to "require peer support" for criminal behavior (Reiss and Farrington, 1991: 376). Apart from their size, it is also well established that delinquent groups are predominantly unisexual (although this finding will be qualified somewhat later), and they appear to be age homogenous as well (Miller, 1974; Stafford, 1984; Sarnecki, 1986; Reiss and Farrington, 1991; Warr, 1996).

Other conclusions about delinquent groups rest on far more limited evidence. As in Sidney's case, it seems that the small groups that commit most delinquent acts are often combinations or subsets of a larger group or clique (Short and Strodtbeck, 1965; Klein and Crawford, 1967; Reiss, 1986; Sarnecki, 1986), implying that delinquents commonly have a larger network of co-offenders than would be expected from the small size of their offending groups. Consequently, one can distinguish between *offending groups* (groups that actually commit delinquent acts) and *accomplice networks* (the pool of potential co-offenders available to an adolescent).

Judging from the limited available evidence, delinquent groups are not highly stable, nor are they highly organized. Evidently, offenders do not ordinarily stay with the same accomplices over long periods of time, and they often belong to multiple offending groups or cliques at the same time (Reiss, 1986; Sarnecki, 1986; Warr, 1996). Within delinquent groups, role definitions and role assignments appear to be unclear and unstable (Yablonsky, 1959; Klein and Crawford, 1967; Stafford, 1984), and shifting membership makes such groups intrinsically unstable. Reiss (1986) has argued persuasively that the membership of delinquent groups is continually subject to change as a consequence of residential mobility, the incarceration of members, and shifts to conventional careers. The result is that "the membership of any group is volatile" and affiliations are "transitory" (1986: 130).

Although there is a tendency toward specialization, most offenders are not exclusively lone offenders or group offenders; rather, they have a history that includes instances of both solo and group offending (Reiss, 1986; Reiss and Farrington, 1991; Warr, 1996). Juveniles with high rates of offending typically have a larger pool or network of co-offenders than low-rate offenders, and high-rate offenders tend to affiliate with other high-rate offenders (Reiss, 1986; Sarnecki, 1986).

In an extensive study of group delinquency, the author (Warr, 1996) examined many of the aforementioned properties of delinquent groups using data from Martin Gold's National Survey of Youth, a self-report survey of a national probability sample of persons aged thirteen to sixteen. Special attention was devoted to three issues: the *longevity* of delinquent groups, the degree of offense *specialization* by groups, and the nature of *instigation* in delinquent groups. The rather lengthy list of findings was summarized in this way:

> Most delinquent events are group events, and there is a strong tendency for offenders to exhibit a pattern as either a lone or group offender. Offenders typically commit offenses with only a small number of co-offenders, but they have substantially larger networks of accomplices, the size of which is proportional to the offender's rate of offending. Offenders ordinarily belong to multiple delinquent groups over their careers and they change accomplices frequently; only rarely do delinquents commit more than a few offenses with the same accomplice. Members of

offending groups are usually no more than one or two years apart in age and of the same sex, although females are more often found in mixed-sex groups than males. It is not unusual for offenders to repeat the same offense with the same group, but offenders are likely to change groups as they switch from one type of offense to another. Groups consequently exhibit greater offense specialization than individuals do.

Most delinquent groups contain an identifiable instigator, a person who is apt to be older, more experienced, and close to other members. Males almost always follow a male instigator, but although females are also likely to follow an instigator of the same sex, they are far more likely to follow males than vice versa. There is a fairly strong degree of role stability within groups, but less so across groups. Most offenders have a history as both instigator and joiner, switching from one role to the other as they shift from one offense or group to another. (33)

One of the principal findings of the study was the short life span of delinquent groups:

According to these data, delinquent groups are short-lived groups, so short-lived that it may make little sense to even speak of group organization. Indeed, if ordinary sociological criteria are brought to bear, it may make little sense to speak of delinquent *groups* at all, at least in any strict sense. The extreme instability of most delinquent groups means that offenders will normally have few opportunities to repeat their role in the same group and thereby develop a stable role structure. And the short life span of delinquent groups can scarcely be conducive to the establishment of group norms or a sense of group identity. Ultimately, the picture of delinquent groups that emerges from these data strongly resembles Yablonsky's (1959) famous characterization of delinquent gangs as "near groups," that is, social units that fall somewhere between organized groups and mobs or crowds. If a defining characteristic of a crowd is its impermanence or absence of history, then these data suggest that offending groups fall more toward the crowd end than the group end of the continuum. (33–4)

Still another critical finding of the study was that persons who are instigators in one group are apt to be followers or joiners in another:

> The fact that frequent delinquents behave as both instigators and joiners strongly suggests that instigation is not a consequence of some stable individual trait, but is instead a fundamentally situational phenomenon that arises from the interaction of group and individual characteristics. That is, adolescents evidently adopt the role that reflects their relative position in the group in which they are participating at the time. When Tom is with Randy and Mike, he is the oldest and most experienced of the three. In his other two male peer groups, he is the youngest. When Tom hangs out with his sister's friends, he is the only male. And so on. (34)

If one were to briefly characterize delinquent groups using this and other research, one might say that delinquent groups are small, shifting, short-lived, unorganized groups of young males. And according to Gold (1970) and others (Briar and Piliavin, 1965; Sarnecki, 1986; Erez, 1987; Cairns and Cairns, 1994), the delinquent behavior that takes place in such groups ordinarily shows little evidence of planning or forethought. Gold reports that 79 percent of the offenses he examined were conceived less than half an hour before they occurred, and 45 percent "just happened" (i.e., no forethought). Similarly, Erez (1987: 183) uncovered evidence of "the remarkably high proportion of crimes of all types committed on the spur of the moment." This suggests that the motivation to engage in delinquency ordinarily arises *after* the group is assembled and as a consequence of group interaction. We will return to this issue later when we consider the nature of peer influence.

DO GROUPS MATTER?

Few, if any, criminologists today would dispute the group nature of delinquency; the evidence for it is simply too strong to be dismissed. What divides criminologists is not whether delinquency is predominantly group behavior but what, if anything, this phenomenon *means*. To some, the group nature of delinquency is a potential key to understanding its etiology. The prevalence of group offending, for example, is sometimes construed as evidence for Sutherland's (1947) theory of differential association or for social learning theories of delinquency (see Chapter 5). The causal importance of peers, however, has been sharply contested by some delinquency theorists on the grounds that the companionship so evident in delinquency is true of most adolescent activities (see especially Kornhauser, 1978). Adolescents, they argue, are notoriously gregarious people; they do everything in groups, including breaking the law. Because the group character of delinquency does not distinguish delinquency from other, legal forms of adolescent behavior, it is argued, it remains unclear whether the group nature of delinquency has any causal significance or is merely epiphenomenal.

The validity of this argument, however, is debatable. Even if most adolescent behavior (legal or otherwise) takes place in groups, it is not clear how this is a damning criticism of peer explanations of delinquency. Young people may be influenced by their peers in all categories of behavior – music, speech, dress, sports, and *delinquency* – and some major theories of delinquent peer influence (Sutherland, 1947; Akers, 1998) expressly argue that criminal behavior is learned from others in the same way that *all* human behavior is learned.

Causal questions about peer influence arise in another way. Proponents of peer influence commonly point to this fact: No characteristic of individuals known to criminologists is a better predictor of criminal behavior than the number of delinquent friends an individual has. The strong correlation between delinquent behavior and delinquent friends has been documented in scores of studies from the 1950s up to the present day (for reviews, see Matsueda, 1988; Warr, 1996; Matsueda and Anderson, 1998), using alternative kinds of criminological data (self-reports, official records, perceptual data) on subjects and friends, alternative research designs, and data on a wide variety of criminal offenses. Few, if any, empirical regularities in criminology have been documented as often or over as long a period as the association between delinquency and delinquent friends.

Those who doubt the strength of peer influence, however, do not question the correlation between delinquency and friends. Instead, they question its interpretation. Drawing on the venerable sociological principle of homophily (people make friends with people who are similar to themselves), they argue that the causal direction between delinquency and friends runs in the opposite direction from that implied by peer influence. People, in other words, do not become delinquent because they acquire delinquent friends; they acquire delinquent friends after they themselves have become delinquent. The most famous proponents of this position were the Gluecks (1950), who aptly and famously described their point of view with the aphorism "birds of a feather flock together."

Today, however, a number of longitudinal studies support the causal direction favoring peer influence. For example, in a simple but telling investigation, Elliott and Menard (1996) examined the temporal priority between delinquent behavior and exposure to delinquent peers within cohorts of National Youth Survey respondents. They discovered that the acquisition of delinquent peers commonly precedes the onset of delinquency, supporting the notion of peer influence as a causal factor in delinquency.

Even if the acquisition of delinquent friends is necessary for the onset of delinquency, however, many criminologists reasonably maintain that the relation between delinquent behavior and delinquent peers *over time* is likely to be bidirectional or sequential. In other words, acquiring delinquent friends leads to delinquency, which increases the subsequent probability of acquiring still more delinquent friends. Thornberry posited such reciprocal effects in what he called his "interactional" theory of delinquency. In a test of that theory, he and his associates (Thornberry et al., 1994: 74) concluded that "associating with delinquent peers leads to increases in delinquency via the reinforcing environment provided by the peer network. In turn, engaging in delinquency leads to increases in association with delinquent peers."

Similar evidence is provided by Matsueda and Anderson (1998), who offer a detailed and careful review of the issue. Still other evidence can be found in Meier, Burkett, and Hickman, 1984; Burkett and

Warren, 1987; Paternoster, 1988; Agnew, 1991; Simons and associates, 1994; Aseltine, 1995; Fergusson and Horwood, 1996; Krohn and associates, 1996; and Reed and Rountree, 1997. What differentiates these studies (inter alia) is the strength of estimated causal effects in each direction. Some find the path from peers to delinquency to be stronger than the opposite path; others do not. However, differences in measures, samples, statistical procedures, lag times, and behavioral domains make it difficult to reach firm conclusions.

A careful and fair reading of the evidence available today, however, permits at least one clear conclusion. Although many investigations offer evidence of reciprocal causation, no study yet has failed to show a significant effect of peers on current and/or subsequent delinquency.

Despite this evidence, the question of causal direction remains a contentious issue in criminology today, largely because it is a principal point of dispute between two major theoretical traditions in criminology – control theory (Hirschi, 1969) and differential association/social learning theory (Sutherland, 1947; Akers, 1998). As a result, many criminologists see the matter in mutually exclusive or zero-sum terms; either peer associations cause delinquency, or vice versa. Outside of criminology, where the matter is less fraught with theoretical animosity, social scientists are more likely to agree that behavioral similarity between peers at any particular point in time is a combination of socialization (i.e., peer influence) and selection (homophily) effects. In one classic study, for example, Kandel (1978) measured the similarity of high school best-friend dyads on two behaviors (marijuana use and minor delinquency) and two attitudes (educational aspirations and political identification) at two points in time (the beginning and end of the school year). She found that behavioral and attitudinal similarity between friends at the latter point in time could be attributed in about equal parts to socialization effects (changes in behavior or attitude among friends) and to selection effects (acquiring new, similar friends).

Perhaps the most compelling evidence on the matter comes from research by the Cairns (1994) mentioned earlier. In their longitudinal study of children in grades four through twelve, these researchers examined socialization and selection effects with respect to a wide variety of characteristics. Summarizing their findings (1994: 117), they report that

> There is strong support for the idea that selection and social-
> ization cooperate over time, as far as our own observations are
> concerned. There is clearly a selection process, where children
> and adolescents affiliate on the basis of sex, race, and socio-
> economic class. There is also a contagion effect, such that once
> the groups are formed, the "selected" behaviors are escalated
> for good or ill. The constraints on escalation typically operate
> from without, in the case of younger children and adolescents.
> Equally interesting, however, is the creation of novel behaviors
> within groups, and their transmission across members. This is a
> particular problem in the case of deviant groups.

The Cairns characterize the social scientific literature on socialization and selection effects in this manner:

> A systematic account of social clusters and friendships must take
> into account the powerful effects of reciprocal influence demon-
> strated in experimental studies and observational analyses. The
> message from these investigations is that reciprocal interactions
> lead to high levels of behavioral and attitudinal similarity, regard-
> less of the initial status of the people involved. The evidence on
> adolescent group dynamics strongly points to the operation of
> both differential selection factors and reciprocal influences. . . .
> Within the clusters of adolescence, strong reciprocal forces oper-
> ate on all members toward conformity. . . . Once in a group, there
> is conformity with respect to a broad spectrum of behaviors and
> attitudes, including shared linguistic and communication pat-
> terns, areas of worry and concern, and "lifestyle" characteristics.
> For many youth, the problem is to escape from synchrony with
> deviant or escalating values. (1994: 128–9)

Criminologists ought to pay close attention to these words, in my view, and abandon the either/or, black-or-white conception of causal direc-tion to which they so often cling.

In a controversy similar to that over causal direction, some crim-inologists have asserted that the correlation between delinquent behavior and delinquent peers is a consequence of measurement errors or artifacts arising from self-report data. When asked to describe the delinquency of friends, they argue, individuals may impute their own behavior to their friends, for example, or impute friendship to people like themselves (see Gottfredson and Hirschi, 1990). Warr (1993a) has raised a number of objections to these claims, and Matsueda and Anderson (1998) have shown that the correlation persists even after accounting for measurement error. What many investigators also seem to overlook is that early studies demonstrating a correlation between delinquent behavior and delinquent peers relied on means other than imputational data (i.e., official records or self-reports obtained independently on respondents and friends – see Reiss and Rhodes, 1964; Erickson and Empey, 1965; Hepburn, 1977), as did a more recent study by Aseltine (1995). Consequently, it is difficult to ascribe the correlation to any alleged idiosyncrasies of self-report data. Whatever it may mean, the correlation between delinquency and delinquent friends seems robust with respect to method.

Questions concerning causality surround all theories, of course, but they have plagued theories and research on peer influence since the moment they first entered the arena of criminology. The reason, I think, is not mysterious. Despite strong and persistent evidence of peer influence in the etiology of delinquency, investigators have as yet failed to identify the precise mechanism(s) by which peers "transmit" or encourage delinquent behavior among one another. It may be true, for example, that having delinquent friends is a strong predictor of delinquent conduct, but that is a little like saying that hanging about swamps increases the chances of contracting malaria. It may be an accurate statement, but it is not particularly informative.

The case for causality would be considerably strengthened if investigators could pinpoint or even narrow the number of mechanisms by which peer influence operates. One of the principal purposes of this book is to organize and describe the ways in which peer influence may act to encourage or facilitate delinquent behavior and to assemble existing evidence that bears on those explanations. It is to this task that we now turn.

CHAPTER FOUR

Peers and Delinquent Conduct

Humans are a gregarious species, and the notion of peer influence is neither difficult to understand nor far removed from everyday experience. Few readers of this book could genuinely claim that their preferences and practices with respect to music, dress, politics, entertainment, or religion were acquired solely from their parents or developed wholly in isolation. Nevertheless, one investigator (Reiss, 1986) was entirely correct when he described the nature of peer influence as "murky."

When it comes to understanding the role of peer influence in delinquent behavior, the principal difficulty confronting investigators lies in the sheer number and manner of ways in which peer influence may operate to encourage criminal conduct. Most criminologists who invoke the words "peer influence" probably have in mind several mechanisms of social influence, and those conceptions often vary considerably from one investigator to the next. My objective in this chapter is to survey the possibilities concerning the nature of peer influence, drawing where possible on existing evidence from the social sciences to inform the discussion and establish a case for each explanation.

The aim, however, is not to champion one explanation over another. Testing and adjudicating among these explanations is likely to require years of concerted effort from social scientists, and it would be premature at this point to select one theory over another. Rejecting

45

a correct theory is no less serious than affirming a false one, and under the present state of evidence the risk of both errors is substantial. Furthermore, it is altogether possible that there are multiple distinct mechanisms of peer influence in everyday life that operate independently or in tandem to encourage delinquent behavior. Consequently, evidence for one theory is not necessarily evidence against another.

With these caveats in mind, let us turn to the task at hand.

FEAR OF RIDICULE

Ridicule is a mechanism of social control in many and perhaps all human societies (Bierstedt, 1957). Though it is often expressed verbally, ridicule may also be conveyed through facial expressions, gestures, laughter, or in writing. The very nature of ridicule is to express contempt or derision for the actions of another, and often, in so doing, to call into question his or her fitness for membership in a group (a family, a culture, the human race, the golf club, or the Vice Lords). Among adolescents, for whom acceptance among peers is often a priceless commodity, and for whom ridicule is a familiar form of interchange (Savin-Williams, 1980), the mere *risk* of ridicule may be sufficient to provoke participation in behavior that is undeniably dangerous, illegal, and morally reprehensible. To risk ridicule is to risk expulsion from or abandonment by the group, or to place in danger one's legitimate claim to be a member of the group. To lose the group is to lose the identity and sometimes the prestige that it creates, as well as the sense of belonging it affords.

The power of ridicule as a mechanism for promoting deviance in groups is suggested by an ingenious study by Beyth-Marom and colleagues (1993). These investigators asked adult and adolescent subjects to list possible consequences of either accepting or declining to engage in risky behaviors (e.g., smoking marijuana, drinking and driving). Of the dozens of consequences, both positive and negative, listed by respondents, the reaction of peers was the most frequently cited consequence (mentioned by 80 to 100 percent of respondents across situations) of *rejecting* a risky behavior (e.g., "They'll laugh at me"), but was much less salient as a reason for *performing* the behavior ("They'll like me"). Avoiding ridicule, it seems, is a stronger motivation for deviance than a desire to ingratiate. Or, as two social psychologists (Kiesler and Kiesler, 1970: 43) have put it, "It is not that we conform just to be liked more. It is often that we conform to avoid being rejected." Beyth-Marom and colleagues also found that teens listed fewer consequences of risky behavior than adults overall, but were more likely than adults to mention social reactions (peers, family, other authorities) at least once. And the investigators found little evidence of logical complementarity in the perceived consequences of behavior; as a rule, respondents produced more consequences for doing something than for *not* doing it. That rule, however, did not apply to peers:

> The most striking deviation from the general pattern was with "social reactions of peers." That possibility was actually mentioned more frequently as a consequence of not engaging in the focal behavior. Most specific instances dealt with potential losses of social standing (e.g., they will call me a nerd; they'll get mad at me). (1993: 560)

Savin-Williams (1980; see also Eder and Sanford, 1986) found ridicule to be the single most common "dominance" mechanism among the young males he observed, far exceeding threats, physical contact, commands, noncompliance, verbal battles, or other mechanisms. So established and familiar is verbal ridicule in adolescent society that the language of adolescents contains terms to distinguish responses to such ridicule, from "taking it" or "eating it" to far more aggressive reactions (e.g., Anderson, 1994).

The sting of ridicule is heightened by the fear of rejection that plagues many adolescents. In a study of British youth, Coleman (1974, 1989) traced a number of adolescent concerns (e.g., conflict with parents, anxiety over heterosexual relationships) over the years separating childhood from adulthood. Fear of rejection by peers, he found, rises rapidly in early adolescence, reaching a peak at about age fifteen before assuming a downward trajectory. What is particularly noteworthy about the age distribution he reports is its resemblance to the age distribution of both peer influence and delinquent behavior it-self, a similarity that in each case may be more than coincidental (see Chapters 2 and 5).

Ridicule is intimately linked to another social practice, gossip, which is often nothing more than ridicule at a distance (Eder and Enke, 1991). By some accounts, gossip plays a pivotal role in group formation and dissolution among children and adolescents, and the threat of gossip seems to operate in much the same way as the risk of ridicule.

> Children's concerns about acceptance in the peer group rise sharply during middle childhood, and these concerns appear re-lated to an increase in the salience and frequency of gossip.... At this age, gossip reaffirms children's membership in important same-sex social groups and reveals, to its constituent members, the core attitudes, beliefs, and behaviors comprising the basis for inclusion in or exclusion from these groups.... Much gossip among children at this age is negative, involving the defamation of third parties. However, gossip takes other important forms. For example, a great deal of children's gossip involves discussion of the important interpersonal connections among children; that is, children discuss and debate whether other children are friends, enemies, dating, and so on. Generally these discussions are not strongly pejorative; instead, children appear concerned with consolidating their separate "social maps" of the structure of the larger group. (Rubin, Bukowski, and Parker, 1998: 639)

Fear of ridicule and gossip among young people is also "fueled by the capricious manner with which in-group and out-group sta-tus can shift at this age" (Rubin, Bukowski, and Parker, 1998: 642) and the fact that adolescents are frequently "haunted by fears of be-ing abandoned and betrayed" (Douvan and Adelson, 1966: 192). In the United States, the transition from the more intimate and family-like environment of elementary school to the larger and more imper-sonal world of junior high school seems to contribute to greater self-consciousness and heightened concern with peer evaluations among students (Simmons and Blyth, 1987: 5–6), adding weight to the power of gossip and ridicule. These two phenomena (along with their close cousin, teasing – see Eder, 1991) may also explain why groups are evidently so effective at communicating their positions to members (Kiesler and Kiesler, 1970), and they may be one reason why adolescent groups seem almost naturally inclined toward unlawful behavior. A suggestion or proposition by one member may be difficult for others to dismiss or refuse, even when they are disinclined to participate.

Stated once again, the power of ridicule stems from the importance that adolescents place on peer acceptance. It is through peers that young persons first establish an identity independent of their family of origin, an identity whose very existence ultimately rests in the hands of *other* people. By risking ridicule, adolescents are in effect risking their very identity, a prospect that few would wish to entertain. If maintaining that identity entails an occasional foray onto the other side of the law to avoid rejection, it may seem a small price to pay to maintain such a valuable possession.

LOYALTY

Loyalty is a virtue and an element of friendship that is readily appreciated by most adults. To remain steadfast to a friend when there are pressures to defect is a cultural motif as old as the Last Supper and as modern as Monica Lewinsky and Linda Tripp.

Criminal behavior raises questions of loyalty to levels that are rarely glimpsed in other domains of life. To be disloyal to members of the group or gang – especially to the point of snitching or ratting on them – is to threaten their freedom, livelihood, and perhaps their very lives. That is probably why trustworthiness or loyalty seems to be the most important trait that adult offenders look for in one another, a trait that, though highly valued, is recognized to be rare – so rare that offenders generally approach one another with distrust (Tremblay, 1993; McCarthy, Hagan, and Cohen, 1998). It is also why snitches fall at the bottom of the prison social hierarchy and why correctional institutions routinely house exposed snitches in segregation units for their own protection.

There is reason to believe that loyalty plays a particularly important role in interpersonal relations among adolescents. Adolescent friendships, once again, are *formative* friendships. They are the first tentative efforts to define an identity outside the family, an identity that may be of enormous importance to a youngster emerging into a new phase of life and a new social world, and an identity whose very newness makes it fragile.

As formative and therefore unpracticed relationships, adolescent friendships often require greater attention to rules and greater clarity and formality in the relationship than will be necessary later in life.` As it happens, one of the most important definitional elements of friendship to adolescents is loyalty:

> In describing the nature of friendship, adolescents typically mention two features not commonly found in children's descriptions. First, friends must be *loyal* to one another; they should not "talk about you behind your back." Commitment and genuineness in attitudes, values, and interests are demanded. (Savin-Williams and Berndt, 1990: 278) [Author's note: the other essential element is *intimacy*.]

> What is needed in a friend at this stage is that she should be loyal and trustworthy – someone who will not betray you behind your back. (Coleman, 1980: 410; see also Youniss and Smollar, 1985; Rubin, Bukowski, and Parker, 1998)

When it comes to delinquent behavior, loyalty means much more than not ratting on your friend(s). It often means engaging in risky or illegal behavior in which one would not otherwise participate in order to preserve or solidify a friendship. Loyalty, after all, can be a potent means of demonstrating friendship, and sharing risky behavior provides an excellent opportunity to prove one's loyalty and seal a friendship (Schwartz, 1987). In a study using national survey data from young people, Warr (1993a) found that adolescents were more likely than either older or younger persons to say that they would lie to the police to protect their friends. Loyalty of this sort may seem misplaced to adults, but their friendships are often less crucial to their lives and identities than those of adolescents. When young persons express mutual loyalty to one another, they create a pact that holds at bay the fear of rejection and isolation that haunts so many of them.

Apart from its importance as an element of friendship, loyalty also provides a form of *moral cover* for illegal conduct. It invokes a moral imperative that supersedes or nullifies the moral gravity of the criminal offense. Yes, I took part in the robbery, but I did so out of loyalty to Sonny, who would have done the same for me. As a universally recognized virtue, loyalty imparts legitimacy to otherwise illegitimate acts and confers honor on the dishonorable.

STATUS

A matter closely related to loyalty and ridicule is the concept of status, a term that denotes prestige or respect within a group. Merely belonging to a group can confer status on an individual, both inside and outside the group, but status more commonly connotes a place within a recognized hierarchy or division of a group.

A tendency to establish status hierarchies in groups seems to be a feature of all primate species, according to Savin-Williams (1980). He reports that young males randomly assigned to a summer camp cabin formed a stable dominance hierarchy within hours after meeting, and that contests over status declined rapidly once the hierarchy was formed. The status hierarchy of the group was mirrored in features as trivial as the sleeping arrangements of the boys, who sought to sleep nearest the alpha male. The boy at the bottom of the status ladder, by contrast, was so utterly inconspicuous in the group that his absence sometimes went unnoticed.

Other research corroborates the claim that status hierarchies form rapidly in groups (see Levine and Moreland, 1990), and it appears that one of the primary objectives of people when participating in groups is to avoid status loss (Cohen and Silver, 1989; Troyer and Younts, 1997). Matters of status seem to suffuse human interaction (Webster and Hysom, 1998), and social scientists have given the topic careful attention (e.g., Berger, Conner, and Fisek, 1974; Ridgeway and Balkwell, 1997).

In one of the earliest and most influential efforts to understand gang delinquency, Short and Strodtbeck (1965; see also Short, 1990, 1997) emphasized the role of "group process" in the gang, by which they primarily meant efforts to earn or maintain status in the gang. Using observational data on Chicago gangs, the authors provided numerous accounts of how gang members sought to acquire status or to fend off threats to their existing status. For example, a gang leader who had been away in detention for some time reestablished his status upon returning to the gang by intentionally provoking a fight with members of a rival gang:

> It is our interpretation that the tough, highly aggressive, behavior was adopted by Duke to clarify the uncertain leadership situation that had arisen as a result of his detention. (1965: 189)

In another instance, an influential gang member, after losing a prestigious pool tournament to another clique of the gang, robbed and assaulted a stranger along with some of his team members. The offense seemed to defy any economic or other explanation at the time, but because robbery was a source of status within the gang, Short and Strodtbeck concluded that

> Gary's action was specifically related to his need for status reaffirmation following the perceived loss in connection with the pool tournament. (1965: 193)

In their efforts to uncover the "status-maintaining mechanisms" (1965: 20) operating in gangs, Short and Strodtbeck focused more on gang leaders than on lower-echelon members of the gang, but their remarks indicate that even rank-and-file gang members derived status through association with the group and/or with highly regarded leaders.

The importance of status in explaining adolescent group behavior can be appreciated only by realizing how precious and fragile a commodity status is among adolescents. Recall that industrial societies deny adult status and its perquisites to adolescents until long after physical maturation has occurred, creating a "maturity gap" (Moffitt, 1993) that persists for years. For many adolescents, the only potential source of status in their lives lies in the world of their age-peers, and the need for acceptance and validation in those relationships, as we saw earlier, can be very strong.

If adolescence carries with it a general problem of status deficiency, imagine what it means to be an adolescent *and* a member of a minority group *and* to live in an economically depressed area. That is the social world described so eloquently and chillingly by Elijah Anderson in "The Code Of the Streets" (1994), an essay on the social rules of the ghetto (see also Anderson, 1999). In the inner city world he recounts, where status is virtually the only possession that many young persons can claim, there is no greater offense than "dissing" (disrespecting) another, especially in front of others, and the penalty for doing so is often immediate injury, even death.

> At the heart of the code is the issue of respect – loosely defined as being treated "right," or granted the deference one deserves. . . . There is a generalized sense that very little respect is to be had, and therefore everyone competes to get what affirmation he can of the little that is available. . . . Many inner-city young men in particular crave respect to such a degree that they will risk their lives to attain and maintain it. . . . The rules of the code in fact provide a framework for negotiating respect. The person whose very appearance – including his clothing, demeanor, and way of moving – deters transgressions feels that he possesses, and may be considered by others to possess, a measure of respect. (1994: 82, 89)

The profound importance placed on respect means that "something extremely valuable is at stake in every interaction" (1994: 92), and consequently even subtle and unintended slights can provoke savage reactions.

> Many of the forms that dissing can take might seem petty to middle-class people (maintaining eye contact for too long, for example), but to those invested in the street code, these actions become serious indications of the other person's intentions. Consequently, such people become very sensitive to advances and slights, which could well serve as warnings of imminent physical

confrontation. This hard reality can be traced to the profound sense of alienation from mainstream society and its institutions felt by many poor inner-city black people, particularly the young. (1994: 82–3)

Ultimately, whether they subscribe to it or not, inner city residents must learn the code in order to survive in the everyday world.

By the time they are teenagers, most youths have either internalized the code of the streets or at least learned the need to comport themselves in accordance with its rules.... [E]ven though families with a decency orientation are usually opposed to the values of the code, they often reluctantly encourage their children's familiarity with it to enable them to negotiate the inner-city environment. (1994: 82, 86)

Long before Anderson's account, Short (1969: 161) observed how social and economic disadvantage feeds a need for respect, and he argued that peer groups fulfill precisely that need among inner city youth:

Peer groups in the lower class often come to serve important *status functions* for youngsters who are disadvantaged according to the success criteria of the larger society's institutions.... Peer groups become the most salient status universe of such youngsters. Group norms and values come to stress means of achievement not prescribed by conventional norms and values.... Delinquency arises sometimes as a by-product and sometimes as a direct product of peer group activity. [emphasis in original]

The importance that adolescents attach to status is often evident in the value placed on status objects – cars, clothing, cellular phones, shoes, caps, and other items that "enhance one's position among peers" (Thornburg, 1982: 198; see also Sullivan, 1989; Short, 1997; Anderson, 1999). Among inner city youth, status is often asserted by controlling access or transit through territory or "turf." Safe passage requires "invitation or an appropriate display of deference" (Sullivan, 1989: 110).

In the end, Muuss (1980: 175) has offered what may be the most trenchant and succinct description of status in adolescent groups:

> The reward system of the peer group (social acceptance, status with the opposite sex, and prestige) appears to be more potent than that of parents and teachers and sometimes even the law. Hence, an individual may feel that the possibility of injury or legal sanctions or even death is preferable to not being accepted by one's peers.

RIDICULE, LOYALTY, AND STATUS

Ridicule, loyalty, and status all seem to be important to understanding interaction within adolescent groups, but what specifically do these phenomena have to do with delinquent conduct? Status, after all, can be achieved through perfectly legal behavior – sports prowess, financial success, academic achievement – and loyalty is commonly appreciated as a virtue rather than condemned as a vice.

The answer, I think, is that loyalty and fear of ridicule are both extraordinarily potent *compliance mechanisms* for inducing conformity in adolescent groups, and they operate to promote conformity *regardless of whether the behavior in question is legal or not.* The same social forces that might lead a group of teenagers to walk a dangerous mountain path, jump into freezing water, or rescue children in a fire, in other words, are the very forces that can lead them to enter a store after hours, share a dangerous drug, or jeopardize their lives by running across a freeway or provoking another group. In the case of illegal behavior, these mechanisms are strong enough to coerce individuals to participate in conduct that they would not otherwise choose to engage in, and which they may personally find to be morally repugnant.

From the vantage point of the group, still another way to think of loyalty and ridicule is as *magnifying mechanisms.* Each transforms the behavior of the one (or a few) into the behavior of the many. Warr (1996; see also Polansky, Lippitt, and Redl, 1950) has offered evidence that delinquent events often commence with an "instigator" who suggests delinquent behavior to others, and it is through loyalty or fear of ridicule that the intentions of the instigator become the actions of the group.

Status is a different matter, however. Rather than merely generating conformity in behavior, status threats (including actual as well as potential ridicule) can provide direct provocation for criminal conduct. Among males, challenges to status often call for direct physical confrontation to maintain identity or "save face" (Felson, 1993). They require an appropriately violent response, a response that, if not put forth, diminishes the status of the hesitant party in the eyes of those who witness or hear of the event.

Experimental studies in social psychology illustrate the dynamics of this phenomenon. In these studies (see R. Felson, 1993; M. Felson, 1994), a research subject is brought into a room to await the beginning of an experiment for which he has volunteered. In the room is another waiting subject who is actually a confederate of the experimenter. In the course of waiting, the confederate addresses an insult to the naive subject, making, for example, a derogatory comment about his dress or appearance. The reaction of the naive subject is then observed and recorded. Characteristics of the situation (e.g., the age and sex of the participants) are systematically varied in these studies to determine their effect on the outcome.

What takes place in these situations illustrates several important elements of confrontational events. First, what is striking about this research is the impact of witnesses to the event. When the two subjects are alone, the insult is often shrugged off or ignored. But when others are present, the reaction tends to be much more aggressive, including not only insults but threats or actual physical attack. These results demonstrate in a clear and convincing way how the presence of others in a situation can be a catalyst for violence. It is for the opinion of the audience, so to speak, that the battle is fought; what would otherwise be merely a private dispute becomes public – and hence objectified – when others are present to witness the event.

The outcome also depends on characteristics of the participants. Males often ignore females or older persons who insult them, but young males are unlikely to ignore other young males. Consequently, it appears that young males are most sensitive to challenges from persons who occupy the same social niche as themselves, i.e., other young males. The use of alcohol also acts to escalate the chances of violence, as does the presence of third parties who actively encourage confrontation.

Students of crime will immediately notice the parallels between these experiments and the actual circumstances that ordinarily precede homicides and nonlethal assaults (see Felson, 1994). Both typically involve disputes between young males in social situations over matters that involve status. It is difficult to avoid the conclusion, therefore, that the operative mechanisms that provoke violence in many real-world situations are our old friends, ridicule and status.

If threats to status can provoke violence, a desire to *acquire* status can also prompt *un*provoked violence from those who engage in "bullying" to achieve status. In fact, it appears that bullies often "seek out situations in which their behavior can be witnessed by their peers" (Felson, 1993: 108). Status also seems to be related to delinquency in another very direct way. As many criminologists (cf. Short and Strodtbeck, 1965) have observed, status in adolescent groups can frequently be earned through delinquent behavior. Why? Because delinquent behavior often exhibits the qualities that adolescent males prize – daring, spontaneity, toughness, leadership – qualities that are valued under other circumstances (e.g., military conflict or emergency rescue) by the larger culture itself. Slaby and Guerra (1988) report that aggressive adolescents expect aggression to enhance their status among peers, as well as their self-esteem. The desire to acquire or preserve status, then, is probably a common reason that members of adolescent groups initiate or participate in delinquent behavior.

Ridicule, loyalty, and status are distinct phenomena, but in the real world they probably do not operate independently, and their relations may be complex. Presumably, all members of adolescent groups dread ridicule because it poses a threat to their claim for membership, and because it may undermine whatever rank they currently enjoy (or wish to attain) in the group. Fear of ridicule, however, probably interacts with status. Those with greater status in the group have more to lose and may take more extreme measures to avoid or thwart ridicule. At the same time, such persons are in a position to *use* or threaten ridicule most effectively to encourage or coerce behavior in the group. As for loyalty, it appears that status can often be earned through genuine loyalty, and the withholding of loyalty is itself a threat to status and may be as powerful as ridicule in prompting compliance. On the other hand, the use (as opposed to the threat) of ridicule is probably incompatible with loyalty in the long run and runs the risk of dissolving or disrupting the group. For while *fear* of ridicule seems to function as a compliance mechanism in groups, the actual *use* of ridicule, as noted earlier, can easily lead to violence. In the real world of adolescent relations, untangling the effects of loyalty, status, and ridicule is likely to be a difficult task.

CRIME AS COLLECTIVE BEHAVIOR

One of the varieties of human behavior that attracts the attention of both sociologists and psychologists is known as *collective behavior*. This category of behavior encompasses the sometimes strange, occasionally violent, and seemingly spontaneous behavior of crowds (riots, panics, looting, mob action, stampedes) as well as other phenomena that involve large numbers of people (the spread of rumor, mass hysteria, financial panics).

Attempts by social scientists to explain crowd behavior have been numerous and varied over the past 150 years. According to LeBon's (1895) famous nineteenth-century account, for example, the anonymity, unaccountability, and invincibility of people in crowds creates a "collective mind" in which crowd members are subject to increased suggestibility and contagious behavior. Among more contemporary accounts, Turner and Killian (1987) have argued that extraordinary events (e.g., natural disasters) that are not governed by everyday rules of behavior often lead to the spread of rumor, the convergence of people in space and time, and the development of "emergent norms" through which "some shared redefinition of right and wrong in a situation supplies the justification and coordinates the action in collective behavior" (1987: 7).

Central to the notion of collective behavior is a simple but profound principle familiar to students of sociology and social psychology for more than a century, to wit, that people will commit acts when they are with others that they would never have committed *if they had been alone* (McPhail, 1991). Persons who could not imagine themselves engaged in looting, vandalism, or attacks upon the police may find themselves doing just such things in a crowd situation, only to return to "normal" behavior afterward. At a more quotidian level, someone who would not ordinarily curse or drink alcohol in everyday life may do so at a party or other social occasion.

Any connection between collective behavior and criminal behavior may seem tenuous at best, but it becomes less so if we remember that criminal behavior is ordinarily group behavior. Many of the leading figures in collective behavior research over the last century have agreed that "practically all group activity can be thought of as collective behavior" (Blumer, 1939: 137), and Festinger, Pepitone, and Newcomb (1952: 382) noted that the "freedom from restraint" that characterizes people in crowds

> is not, however, limited to crowds. It occurs regularly in groups of all sizes and of many different types. For example, a group of boys walking down the street will often be wilder and less restrained than any of them individually would be.

In fact, group delinquency exhibits some of the same traits associated with collective behavior; it is typically unplanned, spontaneous behavior (Briar and Piliavin, 1965; Gold, 1970; Erez, 1987; Cairns and Cairns, 1994) committed by relatively unorganized and temporary (thus, crowdlike) groups (Yablonsky, 1959; Warr, 1996). Applied to criminal conduct, the notion of collective behavior implies that something about the presence of others during an event provides the inspiration (and perhaps the means) to engage in crime.

A full accounting of theories and research on collective behavior is beyond the scope of this book, but an excellent summary and evaluation are to be found in McPhail (1991). Sociologists have made a large contribution to the study of collective behavior, examining the conditions that precede and instigate collective behavior, the composition and varieties of crowds, as well as the forms of communication and mutual action that arise in crowds (cf. Turner and Killian, 1987; McPhail, 1991; Snow and Paulsen, 1992). For their part, psychologists have primarily concentrated their attention on the notion of "deindividuation." In 1952, Festinger and colleagues used that term to refer to a psychological state that frequently appears, they argued, in individuals when they participate in crowds. In this state of deindividuation, persons feel "submerged in the group," and there is a "reduction of inner restraints" (1952: 382) against behavior that would ordinarily be impermissible to the individual.

Following its introduction by Festinger and his colleagues, the concept of deindividuation was taken up and enlarged upon by a number of investigators, including, for example, Zimbardo (1969), Dipboye (1977), and Diener (1977). The thrust of much of this work was to identify the "situational inputs" that give rise to deindividuation and attendant unrestrained behavior. Investigators proposed (and, in some cases, tested) a variety of such "inputs," but there are two that are consistently cited by researchers in both psychology and sociology and that seem potentially relevant when it comes to understanding group delinquency.

Anonymity

The first of these mechanisms is *anonymity*. It seems reasonable to suppose that the fear of observation and detection that tempers everyday behavior in public is often suspended in a large body of people. The apprehension that one might ordinarily feel if smashing a storefront window, for example, would presumably be diminished if dozens of other people in the immediate vicinity were doing the same thing.

Surprisingly, however, anonymity does not seem to have simple, consistent, or especially predictable effects on disinhibited behavior. In reviews of the research (largely experimental) on anonymity, Diener (1977, 1980) reported that subjective anonymity does seem to increase with crowd size, and some forms of disinhibited behavior appear to increase under certain conditions of anonymity (e.g., total darkness). However, he notes (1977: 146) that "anonymity has not always been found to produce unrestrained behavior" and its effects "are quite uncertain" (1980: 222). In addition, Diener cites several studies in which anonymity reduced rather than increased aggression. Investigators, he maintains, often fail to recognize the complexity of the issue. For example, one must ask: anonymity *from whom?* from coactors? from strangers? from authorities? from other disinhibited persons?

Even if anonymity were shown to have a strong and consistent effect in promoting disinhibited behavior, it is not clear that it would apply to much delinquent conduct. Why? Because most delinquent groups are small (typically two to four persons) – so small, it would seem, as to offer little real anonymity under ordinary conditions, and surely less than one would expect in a crowd of, say, several hundred persons.

Diffusion of Responsibility

There is, however, another force at work in groups, one which may be sufficient to encourage unlawful behavior even in small groups. According to research on public perceptions of crime, what most distinguishes criminal conduct from other forms of behavior in the eyes of the general public is its *moral* character. Whatever else it may be – frightening, dangerous, intriguing, tragic – criminal behavior is above all else morally reprehensible behavior.

Several decades of research on the perceived seriousness of crimes has shown that the general public appreciates not only gross differences in seriousness among crimes (e.g., robbery versus shoplifting), but fine distinctions as well (e.g., stealing from a friend versus stealing from a stranger). And there is evidence that the *wrongfulness* (along with harmfulness) of criminal acts is a principal determinant of seriousness judgments (Warr, 1989). What is more, seriousness judgments underlie a wide variety of public perceptions of and reactions to crime, from beliefs about appropriate punishments for different crimes to perceptions of the relative frequency of various types of crime to fear of crime. All this suggests that seriousness is the "master" or overriding feature of crime in the minds of most people.

Criminal conduct, then, is a special class of human behavior because of its deep and intrinsic moral implications, and it is through a moral lens that people normally perceive and understand crime. (Indeed, it is precisely the moral magnitude and complexity of criminal behavior that explains why it is such an enduring subject of literature and popular entertainment.) As for offenders themselves, there is no evidence in criminology that those who engage in criminal behavior are *unaware* of the moral implications of their behavior. They may deny the applicability of conventional moral standards to their own circumstances, and they may have no personal moral reservations about their conduct, but they are surely cognizant of the norms of their own society and of the moral condemnation they risk by engaging in such conduct. Were it otherwise, it would be difficult to explain why offenders are so often concerned with detection by persons other than law enforcement officials (e.g., parents, teachers, or employers; see Jensen and Erickson, 1978). And, in fact, there is evidence that adolescents almost universally anticipate the moral condemnation of their parents if they are caught engaging in delinquency (Warr, 1993b).

How does all of this bear on group delinquency? Moral objections – whether internal, external, or both – ordinarily form a barrier or impediment to criminal behavior (e.g., Wilson and Herrnstein, 1985). According to both sociological and psychological accounts of crowd behavior, one of the primary mechanisms by which crowds remove restraints on behavior is by diffusing the moral responsibility for blameworthy acts. The ethical imperatives that would ordinarily require one to refrain from taking another's property or intentionally damaging a vehicle (or, conversely, that would compel one to help an injured person) can lose their force in situations where the moral responsibility for the act is divided among multiple parties.

Diener (1977) cites several studies that support the diffusion hypothesis, and additional evidence comes from research on what has come to be known as the "risky shift." One might assume that groups ordinarily reach more conservative decisions than individuals, but an extensive body of research commencing in the 1960s showed the opposite; with some exceptions, group decisions tended to be *riskier* than those of individuals (see Shaw, 1981; Friedkin, 1999). There are a number of possible explanations for this phenomenon, but Wallach and his associates (e.g., Wallach et al., 1964) provided evidence supporting the diffusion of responsibility hypothesis and contradicting other explanations. More recent research continues to document choice shifts in groups, but investigators have retreated from the idea that such shifts are consistently riskier than initial positions (Friedkin, 1999).

The diffusion argument seems especially pertinent for explaining criminal conduct because of the extraordinarily grave moral nature of many criminal acts. Much like physical objects, acts whose moral weight would be difficult for any one individual to bear can be borne much more easily by a group – even a small group. Having even a single co-offender, after all, allows one to shift a substantial portion of the blame, perhaps most of it, to another person. For those who cannot bear the moral weight of their own behavior, the group offers a relief from the burden.

There is yet another reason why the diffusion argument may be important when it comes to delinquent groups. In most delinquent events involving groups, there is an instigator or leader in the group – that is, one who suggests or promotes the offense – and that instigator is frequently older (and rarely younger) than others in the group (Warr, 1996; see also Shannon, 1991; Emler and Reicher, 1995). The age difference between instigators and joiners is often small, to be sure, but in the world of adolescents, where a single year can make the difference when it comes to driving a car, buying alcohol, or entering high school, small differences in age are often magnified greatly. To younger members of a group, having an older person present who proposes or encourages the offense may lift much of the moral responsibility from their shoulders while simultaneously granting "adult" legitimacy to their activities (see Moffitt, 1993). In the United States, where adolescent culture is highly age-graded and age-conscious, the greater privileges, experience, resources, and freedom that older adolescents enjoy make them potentially powerful targets of emulation and adulation by younger adolescents (Caspi et al., 1993).

Delinquency as "Rowdy" Behavior

In their detailed study of the daily activities of adolescents, Csikszentmihalyi and Larson (1984) adopted an explanation of delinquency (or, more generally, "rowdy" behavior) that closely resembles the collective behavior approach described here. The authors observed that "there is something about the group interaction of peers that makes rowdiness happen, even if the individual teenagers involved are not inclined to it" (1984: 167), and they emphasized the "group excitement" and "disappearance of personal control" (1984: 170) that takes place in adolescent groups. What distinguishes their analysis from others is the close attention they pay (1984: 168-9) to the temporal aspects of "rowdiness." For example:

> Teenagers reported being rowdy most often on Friday and Saturday nights when they had long stretches of time free of adult supervision. For some it occurred in conjunction with alcohol or drugs; for others it did not.... Teens told of trying to drive an automobile from the back seat and of hanging from railroad trestles while a train passed over. Rowdy activities included driving around yelling, throwing cans on people's yards, and having fights.... After a peak in excitement between 8:00 and 10:00 p.m., they hit a low during the next two hours of 1.0 standard deviation below normal in the feeling of control. By midnight, most of our subjects either went to bed or turned their pagers off, but for those who kept responding, level of control drops to 1.5 standard deviations below the mean.

Csikszentmihalyi and Larson's analysis suggests a close connection between the periodicities of school and home life and the timing of delinquent or "rowdy" behavior.

As a means of explaining the group nature of delinquency, the collective behavior perspective is both powerful and promising. It differs from much contemporary criminological theory in that it employs a situational rather than a characterological approach to crime. As a result, it avoids what attribution theorists have called the fundamental attribution error, or the tendency to attribute human behavior to stable dispositional factors "while overlooking situational causes or transient environmental influences on behavior" (Nisbett et al., 1982: 446; see also Ross, 1977). And it accords with a longstanding school of thought in criminology that holds that criminal motivation is largely situational rather than enduring (Briar and Piliavin, 1965; Gold, 1970; Sarnecki,

1986; Erez, 1987; Cairns and Cairns, 1994), arising most commonly when certain persons (ordinarily young males) come into contact with one another under unsupervised conditions.

In emphasizing situational motivation, the collective behavior approach also accords with evidence that kids who are "bad" in some situations are often "good" in others (Cairns and Cairns, 1994). And as we observed earlier, there are certain undeniable similarities between delinquent groups and crowds. Perhaps more than any other perspective, the collective behavior approach capitalizes on the fact that delinquent behavior is predominantly *group* behavior rather than the actions of solitary individuals.

THE GROUP AS MORAL UNIVERSE

The collective behavior approach to delinquency maintains (inter alia) that groups affect individuals by exempting them, if only momentarily, from the moral code that governs the larger society. There is another way, however, by which individuals may escape or counter the moral rules of their society. As social scientists have long realized, it is sometimes the case that groups *create* their own moral climate; they define what is acceptable behavior within their own self-contained social system. By creating their own ethical reality, they nullify the cultural definitions that exist outside the group and that may control the behavior of those very members in situations away from their companions.

Sociologists and anthropologists ordinarily attribute moral systems to large social units – societies, ethnic or regional subcultures, religious denominations, social movements, and the like. But moral codes emerge whenever two or more individuals enter into social collaboration: a marriage, a partnership, or a friendship. Under such circumstances, the moral "I" is subsumed into the moral "we," and emerging rules of conduct become "our" rules. In joining and sharing their lot with others, individuals establish a new and exclusive moral pact.

The nature and development of norms in groups was the lifelong interest of Muzafer Sherif, who, in a long and distinguished career, relied on both laboratory experiments and naturalistic studies (including the famous Robbers Cave experiments) to observe the development of group norms under everyday conditions and under circumstances of competition, ambiguity, conflict, and the like. In one of his more famous books (*Reference Groups: Exploration into Conformity and Deviation of Adolescents,* 1964), Sherif and his wife, Carolyn, detailed norms in several adolescent groups regarding names, possessions, clothing, loyalty, and group activities (drinking, sexual activity), and they applied the venerable sociological concept of reference groups to understanding adolescent behavior:

> During the adolescent period – the transition betwixt and between childhood and adulthood – agemates in general and one's own associates in particular become major reference groups for the individual. Being in the same boat, they appear more capable of understanding him. They are the ones whose opinions *matter* and whose actions *count*. The "inner voice" which prompts and regulates his social actions is likely to tell him what *they* will think.
>
> When a youth interacts with others of his own choosing . . . he takes part in developing its "customs," its "traditions" (however temporary), and in stabilizing common evaluations of other people, objects and events. . . . They arrive at common definitions of what is good and desirable, how a "good" member *should* and *should not* treat his fellows and outsiders. (1964: 164, 166)

The Sherifs (1964: 182) shrewdly observed how the group can encourage illegal conduct by neutralizing the threat of moral stigma:

> An individual may know perfectly well what his parents, teachers, and preacher say is right and wrong, *and yet violate this without feelings of guilt if his fellows do not condemn him.*

The influence of peers on moral judgment may be particularly acute during adolescence because this period of life coincides with an important stage of moral development. As their store of social experience increases, young people ordinarily come to be aware of the intergroup relativism of moral codes (e.g., Kohlberg, 1964). They recognize that what is permissible in one group (with their cousins, classmates, church friends, or Saturday night friends) may not be appropriate in another. The result is an expanding appreciation of the relativity of standards of conduct.

This relativity figures prominently in the work of Piaget (1932), who in his famous theory of moral development used the everyday reasoning of children (at games like marbles, for example) to adduce a developmental process in which children move from "heteronomous" to "autonomous" morality. In the former stage (typical of children up to about eight to ten years of age), moral rules are perceived as fixed, external "things" that, like physical laws, exist outside the individual, are universally accepted, and are not negotiable or revisable. Through interaction and role taking with peers, however, older children become "aware of possible diversity in views of right and wrong" (Kohlberg, 1964) and eventually come to understand moral rules as internal rules "*constructed* by persons working together in the search for order" (Youniss, 1980; emphasis added) and "arrived at through social agreement" (Perlmutter and Shapiro, 1987: 188).

Piaget described a series of changes in moral reasoning that attend this transition, including an increasing emphasis on intention ("Did he mean to?") over outcome ("Was anyone injured?") in deciding punishment, increasing relativism, a concern for genuine reciprocity, a disinclination toward severe corporal punishment, and other changes. (See Kohlberg, 1964, 1969; Hoffman, 1980; Turiel, 1983; Kagan and Lamb, 1987; and Guerra, Nucci, and Huesmann, 1994, for lucid discussions of Piaget and for subsequent research on moral development).

Piaget's theory, if correct, would seem to have important implications for understanding both the age distribution of delinquency and its group nature. Young persons, who are just coming to realize the moral relativism of the world, may view it as license to engage in *any* conduct, and may revel in the opportunity to create, together with their friends, their *own* moral universe, one free from the strictures of parents, school, and other authorities. Freed from the rigid and simplistic moral rules of childhood, and unencumbered by the more utilitarian rules of the adult world, they can establish a moral code that supplants that of the outside world, granting legitimacy to otherwise illegitimate conduct and suspending or relieving one another of the moral obligation to conform to external social norms.

In a fascinating study of peer influence on moral development, Devereux (1970) reported a series of investigations in the United States and other countries employing the "Dilemmas Test," a structured interview in which young persons (mostly sixth and seventh graders) were confronted with hypothetical situations that pitted peer desires against some "adult-approved or autonomously held standard or value" (1970: 103). In one such situation, for example, subjects were asked what they would do if they went to a movie with a group of friends who chose to lie about their age to obtain half-price tickets. The investigators also measured subjects' "association preferences" (whether they preferred to spend time with their parents, a best friend, or a group of friends), as well as their actual associations.

Summarizing the results of these investigations, Devereux (1970: 109) states that "children who said they preferred peers to parents and groups to friends as spare-time associates, and the children who reported actually spending a good deal of time with a gang of friends were much more likely to say they would yield to peer pressure in such situations," and he concluded that such adolescents are "low on the ability to hold to internalized values when under peer pressure for deviance" (1970: 106).

From these findings, Devereux (1970: 129) ultimately drew the conclusion that exposure to peers is intrinsically criminogenic:

> Children who spend much time with friends yield more to peer pressure than do those who spend much time with adults. And children who spend relatively more time with gangs of peers yield more than those who play with single friends. Hence, at face value, almost any peer experience appears to have at least some potential for drawing children toward deviance.

What makes the research described by Devereux so intriguing is not simply the apparent strength of peer influence, but the mechanism that seems to underlie it:

> Our data indicated that gang [peer] association apparently functioned to *lower feelings of guilt*. . . . Children with extensive gang experience . . . score consistently lower on our measure of guilt following transgression. (1970: 118–19, 130; emphasis added)

Association with peers, it seems, relieves young people from the moral strictures of the adult world, at least in some spheres of behavior. Thus, it is not surprising when Devereux (1970: 137) concludes that "all these findings might be interpreted to mean that peer-group experience constitutes a major roadblock for the moral development of children." And he laments that "as the child grows older...the hold of the peer group increases at the expense of the family" (1970: 137).

The moral support (quite literally) that adolescents can often expect from their peers is evident in self-report data gathered by Lyle Shannon (1991) from two birth cohorts of young males in Racine, Wisconsin. When asked the question, "What did your friends think about the behavior that got you into trouble with the police?," the most common response from these males was that their friends didn't see anything wrong with it. For example, 58 percent of respondents in the combined cohorts whose friends knew of the behavior gave that response about the first reported offense. Another 30 percent said that their friends had no reaction to the behavior.

Even outside their circle of friends, young people are unlikely to face moral condemnation from their age peers. Jensen and Erickson (1978) asked Arizona adolescents what would worry them most if they committed an offense and were "caught and taken to juvenile court." Concerns about parental reactions and about college or job prospects were among the most frequently mentioned worries, whereas fear that "other teenagers might think badly of you" was among the least-cited concerns. One interpretation of this finding is that peer reactions don't mean much to adolescents, but in light of earlier evidence on the importance of peer evaluations at these ages, a more plausible interpretation is that adolescents simply don't anticipate negative reactions from their peers when they break the law.

To some readers, the emphasis here on moral evaluations of conduct will call to mind a branch of criminology commonly referred to as the subcultural tradition. Briefly, this tradition holds that crime occurs because certain social groups tolerate or even approve of criminal conduct (Akers, 1998; Agnew, 2000). Once a thriving area of criminology, the subcultural tradition was seriously wounded by a withering attack from Kornhauser (1978) and her adherents, an attack that drew much of its force from caricature (see Akers, 1998). Be that as it may, the argument here has little bearing on subcultural theory, because it is an argument about the moral reasoning that takes place within small bands of adolescents, and not about the characteristic beliefs of larger cultural groups. The closest parallel that might be drawn between the argument here and the subcultural tradition is the work of Sykes and Matza (1957), who claimed that adolescents commonly draw on a lexicon of excuses, or "techniques of neutralization," to free themselves from the moral burden of what they are about to do. There is some evidence supporting this hypothesis (Agnew, 1994, 2000), although matters like causal direction remain difficult to resolve.

It is worthwhile to note that the arguments in this section are similar in one important way to those in the preceding discussion of collective behavior. The essence of the argument in both cases is that groups provide *moral cover* for criminal conduct. That is, they deflect (anonymity), dilute (diffusion of responsibility), or supplant (with an alternative code) the moral responsibility for illegal behavior. In the latter two cases, these mechanisms operate within the group to alleviate members' own private opposition to the behavior and to counteract the disapproval they face from parents, school officials, police, and others. The critical difference is that, in one case, the moral responsibility for action is merely evaded, whereas in the other, it is denied altogether.

MECHANISMS OF CONSENSUS

In the preceding section I argued that groups can develop their own moral codes, codes that offer moral legitimacy to the activities of the group. And I suggested that adolescents may be particularly susceptible to alternative moral viewpoints because of the phase of moral development that they occupy at that age. In addition, there appear to be social processes operating in adolescent groups that are likely to either (a) generate normative consensus in the group, (b) generate the appearance of normative consensus in the group, or (c) encourage behavioral compliance regardless of any normative (dis)agreement in the group.

What are these mechanisms? There is evidence from social psychology that people ordinarily equate *liking* and *agreement*. Citing the work of Heider (1958) and others, Kiesler and Kiesler (1970: 67) maintain that there is a "tendency on the part of people to perceive that they should somehow agree with those they like and like those with whom they agree." One upshot of this principle is that strong emotional attraction between two or more adolescents can induce genuine attitudinal change as individuals seek to reconcile their beliefs with their feelings for others. This means that even in peer groups where members initially hold disparate moral positions or conflicting stances on factual matters (e.g., the long-term risks of drug use), there is likely to be movement toward consensus in the group.

Another implication of the liking/agreement principle is that people may *feign* agreement with others in order to be liked, because "we apparently think that if we act somewhat like others, they will like us more" (Kiesler and Kiesler, 1970: 42–3). In a fascinating book entitled *Ingratiation*, Jones (1964) employed Goffman's (1959) dramaturgical approach to social interaction and offered experimental data to show how people often feign agreement or approval in order to secure attraction or other benefits. As he put it, "although the ingratiator's own perspective differs from the target person's, he gives signals indicating that he shares the latter's definition of the situation" (1964: 4). Jones discusses tactics of ingratiation (e.g., when to agree, the dangers of "over-agreeing") and demonstrates how strategies of ingratiation mirror the status hierarchies within groups. In an especially ingenious experiment conducted by Jones and associates,

> subjects listened to a dialogue between two other students. One student, Mike, always agreed very closely with the other, Paul, in expressing his opinions on a variety of issues. In half of the cases, Mike went first and Paul second; in the remaining cases the sequence was reversed. In predicting Paul's feelings about Mike, subjects predicted more positive evaluations when Mike expressed his opinions first. They saw Mike as much more conforming and manipulative when his opinions were given in response

to those of Paul. *The opinions actually expressed by Mike were identical in the two cases.* (Jones, 1964: 38–9; emphasis added)

In adolescent groups, whose members commonly share a compelling desire to *be* liked, outward agreement may be used to achieve acceptance by the group, even when there is no overt pressure to agree. Consequently, what appears to be genuine consensus to outsiders and to other members of the group may be merely pseudo-consensus, the illusion of unanimity. Nevertheless, pseudo-consensus of this kind may be as effective in promoting group behavior as genuine consensus, because its existence is known only to (and cannot be revealed by) those who dissent. Matza (1964: 52) spoke of this phenomenon when he described delinquency as a "shared misunderstanding" in which "each member believes himself to be an exception in the company of committed delinquents." The idea of a shared misunderstanding seems especially suitable for describing the kind of unifying but false consensus sometimes found in delinquent groups.

Parenthetically, it should be noted that the other side of the liking/agreement coin – people like those who agree with them – favors the selection interpretation over the socialization perspective on peer relations (see Chapter 3). That is, initial value similarity may serve as an attractor and thus as a selection criterion in the formation of adolescent groups.

Another mechanism that can produce ostensible or actual normative consensus in a group (as well as behavioral compliance) is identified by Kiesler and Kiesler (1970: 33). They maintain that members often fulfill the expectations of the group for the simple reason that "the continuation of the group will be ensured." The importance of peer relationships to adolescents means that they may be willing to feign or even adopt certain beliefs if that is necessary to perpetuate a group in which they find the acceptance they desire. In that connection, recall that delinquent groups are ordinarily small groups, and a significant portion are dyads (Reiss, 1986; Warr, 1996). In small groups, the loss of only one member can mean the termination of the group, and hence efforts to perpetuate small groups may require more extreme forms of compliance or agreement. That fact, coupled with a smaller chance of detection by the police and a reduced risk of "ratting" by accomplices, perhaps helps to explain the small size of most delinquent groups. The irony is that delinquent groups, as we saw earlier, rarely last very long (at least as *delinquent* groups), which suggests that the benefits of the group do not outweigh its risks in the long run.

SUTHERLAND'S THEORY OF DIFFERENTIAL ASSOCIATION

To many students of crime, the very notion of peer influence is synonymous with Edwin Sutherland's theory of differential association, a theory known to all criminologists and one that has been described as a "watershed in criminology" (Matsueda, 1988: 277), the "preeminent sociological theory of criminology" (Gaylord and Galliher, 1988: 165), and a theory that has had "a massive impact on criminology" (Vold and Bernard, 1986: 225).

Sutherland's theory of differential association locates the source of crime and delinquency in the intimate social networks of individuals. Emphasizing that criminal behavior is learned behavior, Sutherland argued that persons who are selectively or differentially exposed to delinquent associates are likely to acquire that trait as well. Sutherland did not limit his theory to peer influence, but tests and applications of the theory have traditionally concentrated on peers rather than on parents, teachers, or others.

The development of Sutherland's theory was a gradual, incremental process. Disappointed with the theoretical chaos in criminology, angered by external criticism of the field, and stimulated by intellectual developments taking place at the University of Chicago, Sutherland pursued a general theory of crime during the 1930s. In 1939, the first explicit statement of differential association appeared in the third edition of his textbook, *Principles of Criminology*. A revised and final version appeared in the fourth edition in 1947, three years before Sutherland's death. The latter statement of the theory took the form of nine propositions, each followed by brief elaborations or clarifications. The nine propositions are as follows:

1. Criminal behavior is learned.
2. Criminal behavior is learned in interaction with other persons in a process of communication.
3. The principal part of the learning of criminal behavior occurs within intimate personal groups.
4. When criminal behavior is learned, the learning includes (a) techniques of committing the crime, which are sometimes very complicated, sometimes very simple; (b) the specific direction of motives, drives, rationalizations, and attitudes.
5. The specific direction of motives and drives is learned from definitions of the legal codes as favorable or unfavorable.
6. A person becomes delinquent because of an excess of definitions favorable to violation of law over definitions unfavorable to violation of law.
7. Differential associations may vary in frequency, duration, priority, and intensity.
8. The process of learning criminal behavior by association with criminal and anti-criminal patterns involves all of the mechanisms that are involved in any other learning.
9. While criminal behavior is an expression of general needs and values, it is not explained by those general needs and values since non-criminal behavior is an expression of the same needs and values.

Detailed discussions of Sutherland's theory are available elsewhere (see Gaylord and Galliher, 1988; Matsueda, 1988; Akers, 1998; Warr, 2001), but a few comments are in order. In contrast with the reigning theories of his day, theories that emphasized hereditary or physiological factors in the etiology of crime, Sutherland asserted that criminal behavior is *learned* behavior, that it is learned from *others* (rather than in isolation), and that it is learned in face-to-face interaction in small, intimate groups (propositions 1 through 3). The *content* of what is learned includes techniques for committing crimes as well as motivation in the form of "definitions" (attitudes) that are favorable to the violation of law (propositions 4 and 5). In the central proposition of the theory (number 6), a proposition that is often identified *as* the theory of differential association, Sutherland asserted that "[a] person becomes delinquent because of an excess of definitions favorable to violation of law over definitions unfavorable to violation of law" (1947: 7). Thus, it is the balance between definitions encouraging and discouraging unlawful conduct that decides whether individuals will engage in crime.

In his remaining propositions, Sutherland stipulated some properties of human relationships (frequency, duration, priority, and intensity) that affect learning, and he advanced what was for the time a philosophically radical position, to wit, that criminal behavior is learned in the same way that *all* human behavior is learned. In adopting this position, Sutherland avoided a common tendency to assume that criminals are a fundamentally distinct category of human beings whose behavior, unlike other forms of human behavior, requires a separate or unique explanation. Sutherland eschewed this point of view, even using as examples of his theory behavior that was not remotely criminal ("a Southerner does not pronounce 'r' because other Southerners do not pronounce 'r'" [1947: 6]). More generally, he observed that "criminal behavior is part of human behavior...and must be explained within the same general framework as any other human behavior" (1947: 4). So strong was Sutherland's commitment to this point of view that he introduced the first published version of his theory with this statement:

> The processes which result in systematic criminal behavior are fundamentally the same in form as the processes which result in systematic lawful behavior.... Criminal behavior differs from lawful behavior in the standards by which it is judged but not in the principles of the genetic [causal] processes. (1939: 4)

Sutherland is not the only criminologist to insist on a general theory of human behavior to explain crime (see Akers, 1998), but his stance was among the earliest and most forceful declarations of that position.

Evaluating the Theory

Tests of Sutherland's theory have conventionally examined the correlation between self-reported delinquency and the number of delinquent friends reported by adolescents. That association has proven to be among the strongest in delinquency research and is one of the most consistently reported findings in the delinquency literature (e.g., Short, 1957; Reiss and Rhodes, 1964; Voss, 1964; Erickson and Empey, 1965; Jensen, 1972; Hepburn, 1977; Akers et al., 1979; Johnson, 1979; Elliott et al., 1985; Tittle et al., 1986; Matsueda and Heimer, 1987; Warr and Stafford, 1991; Warr, 1993a, 1993b, 1998; Dishion, Patterson, and Griesler, 1994; Simons et al., 1994; Thornberry et al., 1994; Matsueda and Anderson, 1998). The fact that delinquency is primarily a group phenomenon also seems to support Sutherland's point of view, although there is nothing in his theory that specifically requires delinquency to be group conduct. That is, one might conceivably *learn* illegal conduct from others but *practice* it alone. Still, the fact that delinquency does ordinarily occur in groups lends support to the idea that it is socially learned.

Despite this generally supportive evidence, there are inherent difficulties in testing and evaluating Sutherland's theory, difficulties that may make it impossible to ultimately reach any firm conclusion about the theory. The major problem lies with the notion of "definitions favorable to violation of law." Sutherland was vague as to precisely what kinds of attitudes or beliefs were to be included under this rubric. Moral evaluations of conduct? Perceptions of the likelihood of punishment? Beliefs about the inequities of life? The possibilities are seemingly endless, and consequently proponents of the theory can always respond to negative evidence by pointing to other possibly relevant definitions. The same problem arises when it comes to terms like "duration" and "priority," which can have more than one meaning and are difficult to quantify or measure (see, e.g., Warr, 1993a).

Over the years, tests of Sutherland's theory have incorporated a variety of different attitudes and beliefs that might reasonably qualify as definitions under the theory, and these tests have produced one consistent result. In most studies, the correlation between subjects' behavior and friends' behavior does not appear to be the result of (or primarily the result of) any attitude transference between individuals (see Warr and Stafford, 1991). Instead, friends' behavior appears to have a *direct* effect on subjects' behavior, suggesting that attitude transference is not the primary mechanism of transmission and raising doubts about Sutherland's cognitive approach to peer influence. Much of the evidence supporting Sutherland's theory is also open to questions about causal direction (see Chapter 3), though that is scarcely unique to his theory.

In the end, Sutherland's theory may well be wrong about the precise mechanism through which peer influence operates. Viewed in proper historical context, however, the theory remains an act of genius, and in its broad features – the emphasis on socially learned behavior, the role of intimates, the parameters of social interaction, the similarities in learning legal and illegal conduct – it was well ahead of its time and may ultimately prove to be correct.

SOCIAL LEARNING THEORY

In 1966, Robert Burgess and Ronald Akers published an influential paper in which they restated Sutherland's theory of differential association in the terminology of operant conditioning, a rapidly developing branch of behavioral psychology associated with B. F. Skinner that emphasized the relation between behavior and reinforcement. In the intervening years, Akers has devoted his career to developing and testing a social learning approach to the explanation of crime, an approach that, like operant conditioning, emphasizes the role of reinforcement (both positive and negative) in criminal behavior:

> Whether individuals will refrain from or initiate, continue committing, or desist from criminal and deviant acts depends on the relative frequency, amount, and probability of past, present, and anticipated rewards and punishments perceived to be attached to the behavior. (Akers, 1998: 66)

Social learning theory benefits from and builds upon the enormous theoretical and empirical development that took place in behavioral psychology during the second half of the twentieth century. As its name implies, what most distinguishes social learning theory from other learning theories is its sensitivity to the *social* sources of reinforcement in everyday life. Capitalizing on the work of Albert Bandura, Akers, and others, social learning theory emphasizes interpersonal mechanisms of learning, such as imitation (modeling or mimicking the behavior of others) and vicarious reinforcement (observing how other people's behavior is rewarded), as well as direct reinforcement, in the acquisition of behaviors. Thus, an adolescent may adopt the delinquent behavior of his friends (e.g., smoking, auto theft, drug sales) through imitation, because he observes the adult status it confers on them in the eyes of others his age (vicarious reinforcement), because it brings rewards like sexual attractiveness and money (direct reinforcement), or because participating in those activities gains him the admiration and respect of his friends (direct reinforcement). Even the simple day-to-day smiles and laughter of peers may be powerful reinforcers for deviance (Dishion et al., 1996). These examples are an oversimplification, because social learning theory focuses on the schedules, quantities, and probabilities of both reward and punishment (see Akers, 1998: 47–89), but they serve to illustrate the broad features of the theory.

Much of the beauty and elegance of social learning theory lies in its generality. Like Sutherland's theory of differential association, it purports to explain legal as well as illegal conduct. And because it uses the same principles to explain all forms of crime, it does not entangle criminology in a thicket of narrow, offense-specific theories of crime.

When it comes to empirical evidence, the generality of the theory has yet to be fully demonstrated. To be sure, the evidence for social learning theory is extensive and impressive (see Akers, 1998), but it is concentrated disproportionately on tobacco, alcohol, and other drug use, and on relatively minor forms of deviance (e.g., cheating). The evidence for the theory, consequently, can best be described as positive and promising, but somewhat limited in scope.

It is the very generality of social learning theory that also makes it difficult to test and evaluate. It is well enough to say that behavior responds to reinforcement, but it is another to actually identify or isolate the precise sources of reinforcement that operate in everyday life. Exactly what reinforcers operate in an inner city gang, a high school drinking clique, a BASE jumping club, or entice groups of teens to engage in vandalism or public nudity? This kind of specificity is what sometimes seems to be lacking in tests of social learning theory. To be fair, the criticism says less about the theory itself than about the difficulties of social science research, and balanced against such criticism is the prospect that social learning theory may ultimately prove to be a means for synthesizing divergent explanations of peer influence into a more coherent, parsimonious form.

CROSS-SEX PEER INFLUENCE

Over the years, investigators have repeatedly observed that delin-quent groups are ordinarily same-sex groups (e.g., Reiss, 1986; Warr, 1996), and that fact suggests that peer influence is predominantly an *intra*sexual process. However, Warr (1996) has presented evidence that qualifies each of those assumptions. Examining national self-report data from adolescents aged thirteen to sixteen, he found that the large majority of delinquent acts reported by males (who commit most delin-quent offenses) did indeed take place in all-male groups. But when he examined the delinquent offenses reported by females, he found that they were significantly more likely to occur in mixed-sex groups than those reported by males. When delinquent events take place, then, fe-males are more often found in the company of males than vice versa. To be sure, it remains true that delinquent groups are predominantly unisexual groups, but that is merely because the majority of delinquent offenses are committed by males (see Mears, Ploeger, and Warr, 1998).

This finding suggests that opposite-sex peers are an important source of influence among females, and, in fact, several studies con-ducted during the past two decades have concluded that, for some females, delinquency is a direct consequence of exposure to delin-quent males. Giordano (1978: 132), for example, reported that girls who spend their time in mixed-sex groups are significantly more likely to engage in delinquency than girls who participate in same-sex groups, leading her to surmise that females learn "delinquent modes of behavior from males." Stattin and Magnusson (1990) discovered that elevated levels of delinquency among females who experience early menarche is attributable to their tendency to associate with older males, who often find them sexually attractive. Warr (1996) found that females were much more likely than males to report that the instigator in their delinquent group was of the opposite sex. Sarnecki (1986: 72) writes that Swedish "girls most frequently became involved with a gang when they were together with one of the boys belonging to the gang." And Caspi and colleagues (1993) observed that New Zealand girls in all-female schools were significantly less likely to engage in delinquency than girls in mixed-sex schools. In these investigators' words, "at least two factors are necessary for the initiation and maintenance of female delinquency: puberty and boys" (1993: 26).

Despite this evidence of *inter*sexual influence, it remains unclear today just how often males contribute to the delinquency of females, and it is also unclear whether the relationships that link male and female offenders are typically romantic in nature or similar to those of same-sex offenders. What *is* clear is that cross-sex peer influence deserves serious attention, especially in light of the fact that peer groups become increasingly mixed-sex in composition as individuals enter middle and late adolescence (e.g., Dunphy, 1980).

GROUPS, DRUGS, AND DELINQUENCY

Most delinquent events are group events, but some kinds of offenses, as we saw earlier, are more likely to be committed in groups than others. Shoplifting, for example, is among the least "groupy" offenses, with a group violation rate of about 45 to 55 percent. By contrast, alcohol and marijuana are used by adolescents almost exclusively in group settings (see Gold, 1970; Erickson, 1971; Erickson and Jensen, 1977; Warr, 1996).

The group nature of drug (including alcohol) use may have important implications for understanding the group nature of delinquency in general because of the strong association between drug use and offending. Evidence indicates that a substantial proportion of criminal offenses are committed by persons under the influence of a controlled substance (Tonry and Wilson, 1990). Some criminologists see no causal significance in this association whatsoever, arguing instead that drug use and criminal conduct merely share some common cause (e.g., low self-control – see Gottfredson and Hirschi, 1990). Others, however, see a causal effect arising from the disinhibiting effects of alcohol and certain other drugs, or via other mechanisms (Tonry and Wilson, 1990).

One can readily imagine several causal scenarios linking drugs, groups, and delinquency. Drug use could be the raison d'etre that brings a group together at a certain time and place, but factors *other than* drug use itself might precipitate delinquent behavior. Or drug use could both unite individuals *and* itself stimulate delinquency. Under another scenario, groups might assemble for reasons unrelated to drugs or delinquency (to try out a friend's new car or to celebrate a birthday), but engage in social/recreational drug use that results in delinquent behavior. Or drug use might simply compound or amplify other processes that naturally occur in groups (e.g., disinhibition). Finally, some groups might engage in delinquency for the purpose of securing money for the drugs they seek.

Although the role of groups in selling and distributing drugs has received attention (Short, 1997), the link between drug *use* and group delinquency is a largely unexplored topic. An exception can be found in Hagan (1991), who offers a variant of one of the causal scenarios just described. Analyzing survey data from Canadian adolescents, Hagan identified two distinct adolescent subcultures, one a genuinely delinquent subculture and the other a "party" culture in which adolescents assemble in their leisure time to attend parties and rock concerts, drive around in their cars, date, and generally pursue "fun and the opposite sex." The only factor common to both subcultures, Hagan found, was drinking alcohol, and he seems to imply that this practice fueled the rebellious behavior of both groups.

Hagan may be correct, but the empirical evidence linking group delinquency and drug use is so scanty at this time that it is difficult to reach any firm conclusions. Given the social nature of drug use, however, and its links with delinquent behavior, it would be foolish to ignore its potential relevance for explaining group delinquency.

BOREDOM

Because adolescents in industrial societies are denied full participation in adult activities and roles, they sometimes find themselves with large blocks of time and little to do to fill them. The result is often boredom, a state for which adolescents are somewhat notorious. As Csikszentmihalyi and Larson (1984: 235) have observed, "boredom is endemic to adolescents because there is much in their life that they do not control."

It seems to be the very nature of boredom that it can be relieved by the company of others (see especially Csikszentmihalyi and Larson, 1984). That fact may help to explain the extraordinary sociability of teenagers and their propensity for delinquency as well. Boredom can lead adolescents to congregate and thereby engage any of the group mechanisms of delinquency described in this chapter. Furthermore, when groups of adolescents are listless, the search for excitement is likely to culminate in illegal activity, activity that may ease boredom and provide excitement for no other reason than the fact that it *is* illegal. The intrinsic features of criminal activity – the danger of discovery and its attendant risks, the interpersonal emotions like trust, shared fear, and mutual protection that come into play – are surely an effective antidote to the monotony of boredom.

Gold (1970) perhaps best captured this process when he sought to explain juvenile delinquency through the analogy of a "pick-up" game. Just as informal neighborhood sports like basketball and baseball offer release from boredom, adolescents looking to "play" at delinquency, he argued, seek out other kids in the neighborhood who can play as well. Gold mentions boredom only in passing, but he emphasizes the fun to be found in delinquency and its similarity to other forms of play. In a similar way, Erez (1987) found that "having a good time," "getting excitement," and "relieving boredom" were common self-reported motivations for adolescent status offenses, and, like Gold, she high-lights the spontaneous, opportunistic, and exhilarating character of many delinquent events.

GROUPS AS PROTECTION

One of the everyday realities faced by some adolescents in the United States is the fact that their school, its surrounding area, and even the neighborhood in which they live are dangerous places, places where the risk of criminal victimization is not negligible. Rates of criminal victimization in U.S. schools are not trivial (U.S. Departments of Education and Justice, 1999), and each day high school students must attend school with a population that is at the peak age of criminality. Nearly all schools contain students who are feared by other students, and according to the Safe Schools Study conducted some years ago (National Institute of Education, 1978), eight percent of junior high school students in large cities said that they had actually stayed home at least one day during the previous month because they feared someone might hurt or bother them at school. One third of those same students reported avoiding three or more locations in the school, the most common being restrooms.

The fact that adolescents often face the threat of violence at school and elsewhere suggests a mechanism that may encourage group formation in daily life. Young people, males in particular, may form alliances and spend their time together *as a means of protection from other males.* The notion of safety in numbers seems almost instinctive in human beings, as it is in many other species (see Warr, 1990).

In his book *Code of the Street* (1999: 91), Anderson describes how the ever-present threat of attack by neighborhood youth forces some young inner city males into pacts whereby

> they informally agree to watch each other's back. When this very strong – and necessary in the inner city – expectation is met, powerful bonds of trust are formed and, with repeated supportive exchanges, ever more firmly established. Essentially, this is what it means to "get cool" with someone.

So strong can these relationships become that young men sometimes assume fictive kinship statuses – "brother," "cousin" – in recognition of their bonds.

In itself, the idea of mutual protection says nothing about the mechanisms that promote group delinquency; but if males form groups for common defense (even though this purpose may be unspoken), the mechanisms described throughout this chapter are apt to come into play and increase the chances of delinquency. By its very nature, the practice of mutual defense calls upon aspects of interpersonal relations (e.g., loyalty) that are likely to facilitate delinquency, and the prospect of intergroup conflict is apt to accentuate matters of status, respect, and dominance, key elements in male violence.

CO-OFFENDERS AND OPPORTUNITY

Most criminologists would concede that, by their very nature, some crimes require group cooperation for their commission, meaning that they depend on look-outs, extra labor, collective intimidation or defense (e.g., strongarm robberies, holding hostages), or accomplices with specialized skills. For some subset of crimes, then, the availability of co-offenders seems to constitute a necessary condition for crime. This means that group offending can be analyzed from the perspective of opportunity theories of crime, theories that emphasize the convergence in time and space of necessary conditions for crime (see Cohen and Felson, 1979; Warr, 2002). In what is perhaps the most famous such theory, Cohen and Felson (1979) argued that criminal events depend on the convergence of motivated offenders, suitable targets, and the absence of capable guardians, and they demonstrated how historical changes in these variables (for example, a long-term decline in the guardianship of homes stemming from increasing labor force participation among women and a rising number of one-person households) affect crime rates.

Viewed from an opportunity perspective, the simple *availability* of co-offenders can be understood as an opportunity for crime in circumstances where accomplices are essential. In that case, the opportunity to engage in crime depends not merely on the activities of any one person, but on the interconnecting activities of *several* people. Whether Alex gets into trouble today, in other words, depends not only on his free time, but also on whether his friends are occupied with work, studying, household chores, or other friends. If three friends each have a one in ten chance that they will be available on any particular day, and if these probabilities are independent, then the likelihood that all three are available for crime on a given day is only 1 in 1,000 (see Felson, 1994; Warr, 2002). Understanding delinquent events therefore becomes an exercise in understanding the coordination of activities among adolescents (do they attend the same school, ride the same bus, share the same work schedule, or eat lunch at the same sandwich shop?). As necessary conditions for crime, opportunities are also *limiting conditions,* meaning that they define the maximum possible frequency of a crime (Warr, 2002). Accordingly, where co-offenders are a necessary condition for crime, it becomes essential to understand their availability for that purpose.

The availability of co-offenders might seem to be unproblematic, especially if one assumes a subcultural view of delinquency (Tremblay, 1993). But the matter is not as straightforward as it seems. Reiss and Farrington (1991), for example, demonstrated that propinquity, along with homophily, was an important element of co-offender selection in their sample of London males (especially among younger offenders), suggesting that mobility and the *local* availability of age (and ethnic) peers are significant constraining influences on delinquency. In another study of co-offending, Warr (1996) showed that adolescent offenders typically accumulate a fairly large list of co-offenders by the age of sixteen, but that they rarely commit more than one or two offenses with any one of those co-offenders. This pattern may simply reflect the constantly shifting nature of adolescent friendships, but it is so pronounced as to suggest that delinquents actively *avoid* prolonged contact with any one accomplice, perhaps because of the risk of mutual exposure it creates. In any event, the point is that the immediate supply of co-offenders available at any particular time appears to be more limited than the accumulated pool of accomplices would suggest.

Among older, more seasoned offenders, the "search for co-offenders" (Tremblay, 1993) appears to be an especially important aspect of opportunity. Aside from actual accomplices during the commission of crimes, offenders often have "contacts" and "connections" with fences, tipsters, prostitutes, former cellmates, bail bondsmen, and members of certain criminal markets (e.g., stolen credit cards or drugs) who are valuable for identifying, carrying out, and disposing of scores. Tremblay (1993: 19) notes that the very definition of "suitable targets" for crime depends on the market(s) to which an offender is tied. As noted earlier, the principal characteristic that offenders search for in their colleagues seems to be trustworthiness, a trait that is highly valued but recognized to be rare, so rare that offenders generally approach one another with distrust (Tremblay, 1993; McCarthy, Hagan, and Cohen, 1998).

Participating in criminal networks can significantly increase opportunities for crime, because the opportunities known to or available to one individual (e.g., access to drugs, knowledge about cash deliveries at a bank chain) become available to others. Ultimately, what sets the availability of co-offenders apart as a form of opportunity is the fact that criminal events often depend not on the activities of any one individual, but on the intersections between the criminal careers of numerous offenders. Viewed that way, opportunity is not only temporally and spatially structured, but *socially* structured as well, and opportunities for crime have as much to do with relations among offenders as with those between offenders and victims.

THE VIRTUAL PEER GROUP

As we saw in Chapter 2, contact with peers during childhood and adolescence has been limited in some societies and during some historical periods. During the last century, however, technological developments have greatly increased opportunities for communication among adolescents. The advent of the telephone as a household consumer appliance in the United States facilitated real-time communication among teenagers outside of school (see Crockett, Losoff, and Petersen, 1984), a fact known to all (and lamented by many) parents of teenagers. The development of the cellular phone has made communication easier still. The automobile, as we have seen, overcame obstacles of distance that restricted face-to-face contact among adolescents. Today the internet offers round-the-clock communication with friends and strangers in age-segregated "chat rooms" and other forums that know few geographic boundaries. The social possibilities of this communication medium were brought home to me one day as I watched one of my sons play a computer game with a friend over the internet, a game in which each player could see and speak to the other's character (or "avatar") on the screen, and could choose to fight him or cooperate with him against other players. The result was a kind of live childhood adventure taking place in an imaginary but *socially* real universe.

Along with these major twentieth-century improvements in communication came changes in vicarious communications as well. Motion pictures found an eager audience among teenagers beginning in the 1950s, foreshadowing the many age-targeted movies of today, and magazines and music tailored specifically to teenage tastes arrived at about the same time. Today, with the help of television channels devoted solely to those their own age (e.g., MTV), adolescents can immerse themselves in the world of their peers with little or no outside interruption.

What do these facts have to do with peer influence? In many ways, the mass media offer modern adolescents a *virtual peer group,* a group with which they can identify socially and psychologically, from which they can assimilate tastes and norms of dress, speech, and sexuality, and within which they can develop a self. There is no evidence as yet that such virtual peer groups have replaced or supplanted real ones, but no one who visits the United States can fail to be struck by the remarkable similarity among adolescents who live thousands of miles apart in highly disparate communities and climes, or by teenagers who seem to include fictional television characters in their real-life reference groups.

The impact of the mass media on human behavior is a matter too large and complex for close attention here, but there are reasons to suspect that it is not negligible. The emphasis placed on modeling in social learning theory seems to be justified, and television, movies, and other mass media offer a variety of attractive peer models to adolescents, surrounding them with a glamour that real life seldom achieves. Then, too, time spent with the virtual peer group is time *not* spent talking or interacting with parents and other adults (Coleman and Hoffer, 1987; Warr, 1993b). What perhaps most differentiates the virtual peer group from real peer groups is that it is available nearly everywhere (at least in the United States) at all times – late at night, on holidays, weekends, and summer vacation, and when real friends are sick or working. It is as close as the nearest television, computer, or set of headphones, which for many adolescents is no farther than their backpack or bedroom.

As for delinquent behavior, it is perhaps unnecessary to add that the peers one meets in the virtual peer group are not always law-abiding or nonviolent. The preoccupation of the mass media with crime and violence borders on the obsessive (see Warr, 2000), and consequently the virtual peer group often contains an ample supply of dubious role models.

SUMMARY

The goal of this chapter has been to set forth some possible mechanisms by which peers contribute to delinquency. I have sought to make the strongest possible case for each mechanism and to marshal existing evidence in each instance. Some readers will be frustrated by the sheer number of possibilities and by my reluctance to adopt one or the other as a favored explanation. As I noted at the outset of the chapter, however, it is premature to attempt to narrow the possibilities under the present state of research. Nevertheless, it is a significant step forward, in my view, simply to enumerate and describe the possible mechanisms that fall under the oft-used rubric of "peer influence." As things stand today, that phrase continues to be used to hide an appalling lack of knowledge about how peers promote delinquency. With time and sufficient research, some of these contenders will drop from the competition, while others will remain standing, and the phrase "peer influence" will take on a clearer and more empirically defensible connotation.

CHAPTER FIVE

Applying Peer Explanations of Delinquency

The preceding chapter described a variety of possible mechanisms of peer influence and offered some grounds for treating peers as an important element in the etiology of delinquency. This chapter extends the case for peer influence further by demonstrating how peer variables can help to explain some of the most fundamental features of delinquent behavior. It also contrasts the strength of peer influence with another very powerful source of influence in the lives of adolescents – the family.

AGE AND CRIME

One of the most indisputable features of criminal behavior is its age distribution. Though a seemingly mundane phenomenon, the age distribution of criminal behavior is intriguing enough to have caught the attention of Quetelet, the Gluecks, Sutherland, and, in more recent times, Hirschi and Gottfredson, Sampson, Blumstein, Farrington, and others.

What so arouses the attention of criminologists is the lawlike relation between age and criminal conduct. According to all major methodologies for measuring crime (self-reports, official data, and victimization data), age-specific rates of offending in the general population peak in middle to late adolescence for most offenses, and drop sharply and permanently thereafter (Hirschi and Gottfredson, 1983; Wilson and Herrnstein, 1985; Farrington, 1986; Blumstein and Cohen, 1987; Wolfgang, Thornberry, and Figlio, 1987; Steffensmeier et al., 1989; Moffitt, 1993). Drug offenses are one of the few exceptions to this rule, reaching a peak at later – but still early – ages (Bachman et al., 1984; Kandel and Yamaguchi, 1987; Akers, 1992).

In recent years, the relation between age and crime has emerged as one of the dominant issues in criminology, thanks in large part to a single publication. In 1983, Hirschi and Gottfredson's seminal article entitled "Age and the Explanation of Crime" launched an era of research on the age/crime relation. The authors advanced strong and controversial ideas, most notably the assertion that the age distribution of crime is historically, culturally, and demographically invariant. That claim has not gone unchallenged (Greenberg, 1985; Blumstein, Cohen, and Farrington, 1988; Steffensmeier et al., 1989) but neither has it gone undefended (Gottfredson and Hirschi, 1988, 1990; Britt, 1994).

Another, equally strong assertion was Hirschi and Gottfredson's (1983: 554) claim that "the age distribution of crime cannot be accounted for by any variable or combination of variables currently available to criminology." In a later statement of this position, Gottfredson and Hirschi (1990: 124) pointed more directly to sociological explanations: "With the failure of sociological theories to explain the variables they were originally designed to explain, . . . their utility as explanations of the large correlates of crime – age, gender, and race – [are] no longer plausible."

The difficulties that arise in explaining the association between age and crime are indeed daunting. Chief among them is the fact that any explanation must account for seemingly contrary phenomena, i.e., the rapid onset *and rapid desistance* from crime that for most offenses is centered in the middle to late teens. "Just at the point where the criminal group has been created, it begins to decline in size" (Gottfredson and Hirschi, 1990: 131). In addition, the age gradient of crime is so steep that it requires from any explanation rather profound age-related changes in the explanatory variables.

Notwithstanding the claims of Gottfredson and Hirschi, it is possible that the age distribution of crime is in fact a consequence of social factors, specifically, changes in peer relations over the life course. If peer influence does account in any way for the age distribution of crime, then one would expect to observe substantial and rapid changes in peer relations from one age group to another.

Figure 5.1 comes from a study conducted by the author (Warr, 1993a) that pooled data from five consecutive annual waves of the National Youth Survey (NYS). The NYS is an ongoing longitudinal study of a national probability sample of 1,726 persons aged eleven to seventeen in 1976 (see Elliott et al., 1985), and it is among the largest and most comprehensive data sets ever assembled by criminologists. In each wave of the NYS, respondents are asked this question: "Think of the people you listed [earlier in the interview] as close friends. During the last year how many of them have (act)?" (1 – none of them, 2 – very few of them, 3 – some of them, 4 – most of them, 5 – all of them). The question is asked about a variety of offenses, including vandalism, cheating, marijuana use, petty theft, alcohol use, burglary, selling hard drugs, and grand theft.

Figure 5.1 depicts the relation between age and exposure to delinquent peers by showing the percentage of respondents by age and offense who report that *none* of their friends has committed the act in question during the prior year. The first plot pertains to marijuana use, and it paints a startling picture. At age eleven, fully 95 percent of respondents report that none of their friends has smoked marijuana. Five years later, at age sixteen, that figure has dropped to 40 percent, and at age eighteen it hovers at only 25 percent. The decline from one age group to the next thus averages about 10 percent per year. The next plot shows even more dramatic figures for alcohol use. At age eleven, approximately nine out of ten respondents (87 percent) report that none of their friends has used alcohol during the past year. Five years later, at age sixteen, the figure is merely 18 percent, falling yet further to 8 percent by age eighteen. The decline across age groups in the percentage of unexposed adolescents is so great as to literally be exponential.

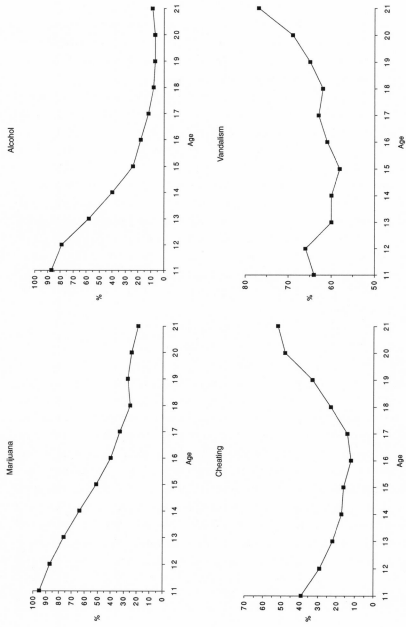

Figure 5.1. Percentage of respondents with no delinquent friends, by age and offense.

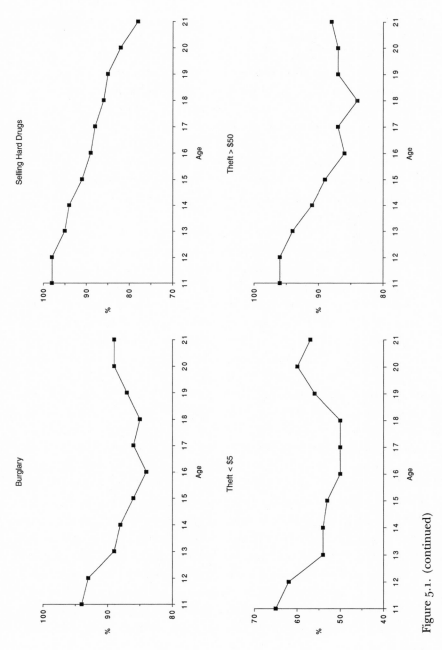

Figure 5.1. (continued)

95

The plots for alcohol and marijuana use are distinctive not only for the magnitude of change they exhibit, but also for their general shape. For both offenses (and for selling hard drugs as well), there is no significant decrease in the number of delinquent peers as respondents approach age twenty-one, meaning that the peak age of peer involvement lies somewhere above that age. This pattern is consistent with self-report studies of the age distribution of alcohol and drug use (Bachman et al., 1984; Kandel and Yamaguchi, 1987; Akers, 1992). Of the remaining plots, however, all show a different pattern, with peer involvement peaking in the middle to late teens and declining thereafter. These plots, too, are consistent with self-report data on the age distribution of most nondrug delinquent offenses (Farrington, 1986; Steffensmeier et al., 1989).

The evidence in Figure 5.1 points to a clear and compelling conclusion: During adolescence, individuals frequently undergo rapid and enormous changes in exposure to delinquent peers, from a period of relative innocence in the immediate preteen years to a period of heavy exposure in the middle to late teens. This intense exposure to delinquent peers begins to decline, however, for many but not all offenses, as individuals leave their teens and enter young adulthood.

Exposure to delinquent peers, however, is not the only element of peer relations that changes dramatically during adolescence. In each wave of the NYS, respondents were asked, "How many evenings in an average week, including weekends, have you gone on dates, to parties, or to other social activities?" Figure 5.2 shows the percentage of respondents, by age, who report that they average three or more nights per week in such activities. The plot reveals a rapid increase with age in the amount of *time* spent with peers, from a low of 12 percent among eleven-year-olds to a peak of 52 percent among eighteen-year-olds. After that age, time spent with peers drops rapidly, reaching 32 percent by age twenty-one. Another element of peer relations is the *importance* that individuals place on activities with peers. In the NYS, respondents were asked, "How important has it been to you to have dates and go to parties and other social activities?" (1 – not important at all, 2 – not too important, 3 – somewhat important, 4 – pretty important, 5 – very important). Figure 5.3 shows the proportion of respondents, by age, who reported that these activities were "pretty important" or

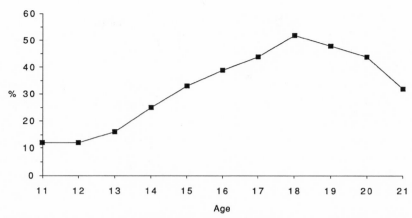

Figure 5.2. Percentage of respondents reporting that they averaged three or more nights per week going "on dates, to parties, or to other social activities," by age.

"very important." The range in this proportion (19 percent) is not as great as in the preceding plot, but the shape of the plot is quite similar. The importance of peer relations peaks at age seventeen, and shows a rather steep descent thereafter. It seems that friends begin to lose their central importance to many adolescents before they actually begin to disassociate themselves from them.

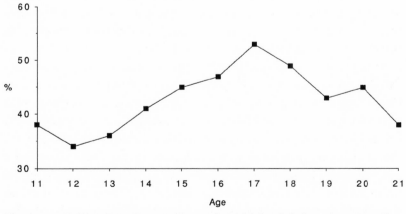

Figure 5.3. Percentage of respondents who said that it is "very important" or "pretty important" to "have dates and go to parties and other social activities," by age.

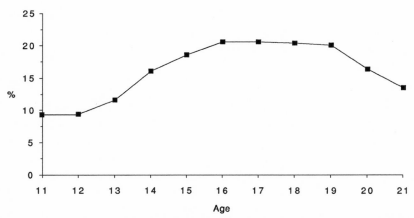

Figure 5.4. Percentage of respondents who said that they would lie to protect their friends if they got into trouble with the police, by age.

The NYS also asks respondents several questions about their *loyalty* to their friends (see Chapter 4), i.e., how the respondent would react if "your group of friends was leading you into trouble." The most well-behaved item, and the most relevant for present purposes, questions respondents about how they would react to illegal behavior on the part of their friends: "If your friends got into trouble with the police, would you be willing to lie to protect them?" (1 – no; 2 – yes). Figure 5.4 shows that respondents aged sixteen to nineteen are about twice as likely as their younger or older counterparts to respond affirmatively to this question, meaning that their loyalty to their friends extends even to concealing illegal behavior.

The evidence presented in Figures 5.1–5.4 is quite consistent with the developmental changes during adolescence discussed in Chapter 2. The relevance of peers in the lives of young persons reaches its zenith in the middle to late teens. Age-related changes in the importance of peers, the amount of time spent in their company, and loyalty to peers are substantial, so much so that they could reasonably be expected to exert strong, even profound, effects on the behavior of adolescents. And like the age distribution of crime itself, the role of peers is transitory, rising and falling quickly during a relatively brief period of life.

Even if all these observations are true, it does not necessarily mean that peer variables account for the age distribution of crime. The final portion of this study, however, provided evidence on the most important piece of the puzzle. When measures of peer influence were held constant, the association between age and crime was substantially weakened, and for some offenses it disappeared entirely. Judging from this evidence, it appears that *the age distribution of crime stems primarily from age-related changes in peer relations,* changes that are part of the ordinary developmental process that takes place during adolescence. Far from being an impenetrable conundrum, the age/crime relation seems to require no "special" explanation but is instead a result of one of the most distinctive and best-known features of adolescence.

PEERS AND THE LIFE COURSE

The rise of interest in the age/crime relation coincided with, and was perhaps mutually stimulated by, another development, that is, a growing concern with life-course approaches to criminal behavior. Setting aside the traditional preoccupation with interindividual differences in criminality, the life-course perspective concentrated on changes in criminality *within* individual biographies as persons progressed from childhood through adolescence, adulthood, and old age and experienced major life-course transitions like marriage, employment, and childbirth.

Spurred in part by the "criminal career" perspective in criminology (Blumstein, Cohen, and Farrington, 1988), the success of the life-course paradigm in sociology (Elder, 1985), and the growing influence of developmental psychology in criminology (e.g., Thornberry, 1997), the life-course approach was further stimulated by the dramatic theoretical confrontation between so-called ontogenetic and sociogenetic theories of crime (Sampson and Laub, 1993; Cohen and Vila, 1996; Matsueda and Heimer, 1997). The former assert that the propensity to engage in crime is present at an early age, is stable through life, and consequently is unaffected by events that occur in life. The latter maintain that life-course events like marriage, full-time employment, college attendance, and entry into the military have a pronounced affect on criminal careers. To date, evidence from empirical studies has generally favored the sociogenetic point of view (Sampson and Laub, 1993; Warr, 1993a, 1998; Bartusch et al., 1997; Paternoster and Brame, 1997; Simons et al., 1998; Uggen, 2000; but see Nagin and Farrington, 1992a, 1992b; Nagin and Land, 1993).

The shift toward the life-course approach within criminology was encouraged by the publication of an influential book by Robert Sampson and John Laub entitled *Crime in the Making: Pathways and Turning Points in Life* (1993). Arguing that criminologists had narrowly fixated on the teenage years, Sampson and Laub sought to bring "both childhood and adulthood back into the criminological picture of age and crime" (1993: 7). To that end, they adopted the conceptual tools of the life-course perspective (Elder, 1985) and the etiological principles of control theory (Hirschi, 1969; Durkheim [1897] 1951). Strong ties to age-linked institutions of social control – family, school, and peers in childhood and adolescence; higher education, marriage/parenthood, work and community in adulthood – inhibit deviant behavior, they argued, and changing ties to these institutions over the life course produce distinctly different criminal *trajectories* marked by *turning points* (changes in the life course) from conventional to criminal behavior and vice versa.

To test their thesis, Sampson and Laub revived data from the Gluecks' well-known longitudinal study of delinquents, data that were initially collected in 1939 and that had lain dormant since the 1950s. The Glueck data, as the authors rightly observed, were notable not only for their longitudinal character, but also for the rich variety of variables and sources (self-reports, parent and teacher reports, official data) that they encompassed. Briefly stated, Sampson and Laub's reanalysis of the Gluecks' data led them to claim substantial support for their position. For example, they found that marital attachment and job stability had significant effects in reducing deviant behavior during adulthood, even among those with a history of delinquency in childhood or adolescence.

Sampson and Laub's investigation is among the most comprehensive and sociologically sophisticated analyses of criminal careers ever undertaken. Yet, despite the care and skill they brought to the task, their analysis suffered from a serious flaw. In advancing their control explanation of desistance, Sampson and Laub failed to acknowledge or test a rival explanation of their findings, one that is not only possible but highly plausible.

To illustrate, consider the impact of marriage on desistance from crime. Sampson and Laub (1993: 140) write that "the structural institution of marriage per se does not increase social control. However, strong attachment to a spouse (or cohabitant) combined with close emotional ties creates a social bond or interdependence between two individuals that, all else being equal, should lead to a reduction in deviant behavior." They further elaborate that "adults, regardless of delinquent background, will be inhibited from committing crime to the extent that they have social capital invested in their work and family lives. . . . By contrast, those subject to weak systems of interdependence and informal social control as an adult . . . are freer to engage in deviant behavior – even if nondelinquent as a youth." (141)

These statements are a straightforward summary of control theory – strong ties to conventional institutions or persons create stakes in conformity and thereby inhibit deviance (Hirschi, 1969). But marriage may discourage deviance for an altogether different reason. If delinquency is indeed a consequence of peer influence, then marriage takes on special significance as a potential cause of desistance from crime. Specifically, if delinquency stems from association with delinquent friends, and if marriage disrupts or dissolves relations with those friends and accomplices, then marriage ought to encourage desistance from crime. The predicted outcome – marriage leads to desistance – is of course the same under either explanation, but the social mechanism that produces that outcome is fundamentally different.

Evidence for a peer explanation of desistance comes from several sources. Knight and West (1975) divided a small group of British delinquents into two groups: those who had no further criminal convictions or self-reported offenses after age sixteen (*temporary delinquents*) and those who continued to commit offenses after that age (*continuing delinquents*). Among those who had desisted from crime (temporary delinquents), more than half reported that "they had abandoned the

male peer groups of their adolescent, delinquent phase" (1975: 45).
As one offender put it, "'To keep out of trouble, that's why I don't go
round them no more. . . . I don't hang around with a lot of mates or
anything like that.'" By contrast, those who had not desisted (continuing delinquents) showed no decline in their level of peer involvement
as they grew older.

As we saw earlier, measures of peer influence – the amount of time
that adolescents spend with their friends, their exposure to delinquent
friends, and their commitment to friends – peak in the middle to
late teens, producing an age curve that is strikingly similar to the
age curve of most delinquent offenses. What remains unclear, however, is *why* peer relations decline in importance as adolescents enter
adulthood.

In a study responding to the research of Sampson and Laub, I sought
to determine whether links between major life-course transitions and
desistance from crime can be attributed to changing relations with
peers (see Warr, 1998). Using data from the National Youth Survey
once again, the investigation concentrated on one major life-course
transition – marriage – and its role in encouraging desistance from
crime. In particular, the objective was to determine whether the effect of marriage on desistance can be attributed to any disruption or
dissolution of peer relations that accompanies marriage.

The data in Table 5.1, reproduced from this study, reveal a marked
contrast between married and unmarried individuals. More than half
(56.8 percent) of married respondents eighteen to twenty-four years
old report that they spend no more than one weekday evening each
week with friends. By contrast, only a fifth (19.9 percent) of single respondents report such infrequent contact ($X^2 = 164.45$, 5 df,
$p < .0001$). Indeed, more than a third (35.4 percent) of single respondents indicate that they spend *all* or nearly all (four out of five)
weekday evenings with friends, compared to only one in thirteen married respondents (7.8 percent). Much the same pattern holds for afternoon and weekend time. Unmarried respondents are nearly four
times as likely (37.9 versus 9.9 percent) to report that they spend four
or five afternoons a week with friends ($X^2 = 125.28$, 5 df, $p < .0001$).
And married respondents are 2.5 times more likely than single

Table 5.1. *Time spent with friends each week, by marital status*

	Weekday evenings (%)							
	0	1	2	3	4	5	Total	(N)
Unmarried	6.4	13.5	21.6	23.1	17.1	18.3	100.0	(1,068)
Married	15.6	41.2	23.5	11.9	4.5	3.3	100.0	(243)

	Weekday afternoons (%)							
	0	1	2	3	4	5	Total	(N)
Unmarried	11.3	12.2	18.0	20.7	13.3	24.6	100.0	(1,069)
Married	25.9	30.5	19.8	14.0	4.1	5.8	100.0	(243)

	Weekend time (%)						
	Very little	Not too much	Some	Quite a bit	A great deal	Total	(N)
Unmarried	3.8	7.6	23.6	38.2	26.7	100.0	(1,070)
Married	9.1	19.8	37.4	25.5	8.2	100.0	(243)

respondents to say that they spend "very little" or "not too much" time on the weekends with friends ($X^2 = 93.57$, 4 df, $p < .0001$).

Figure 5.5 elaborates on Table 5.1 by showing the relation between time spent with friends and the precise person(s) with whom respondents were living (i.e., parents/step-parents, spouse, roommate, opposite sex, alone). Only evening time is shown here, but the pattern is similar for afternoon and weekend time. Examination of Figure 5.5 reveals that persons who live with a spouse are distinctly different from those in other household arrangements. Among those living with a spouse, time spent with friends peaks sharply at one night per week and drops rapidly thereafter. By contrast, the modal category for most of the remaining household types is two or three nights per week, and there are substantially more persons in those households who average four or five weekday nights each week with friends.

The data in Figure 5.5 demonstrate that it is not merely those who live at home with their parents who spend much of their time with friends. The same is true for those who have *left* home but remain

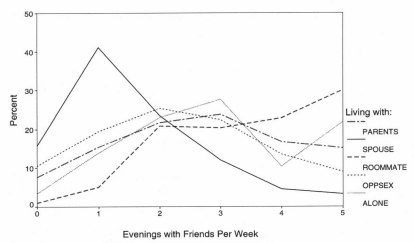

Figure 5.5. Evenings spent with friends per week, by household composition.

unmarried (i.e., those who live alone, with one or more roommates, or who are cohabiting). Consequently, it appears that there is something about marriage itself – not simply leaving home or even cohabitation – that affects relations with friends.

The data in Table 5.1 and Figure 5.5 are cross-sectional, but longitudinal evidence on marriage and time spent with peers reveals a similar pattern. Figure 5.6 shows changes in the amount of time (afternoon, evening, or weekend) spent with friends among two groups of respondents: those who remained unmarried at both waves 5 and 6 of the NYS (left plots), and those who were unmarried at wave 5 but who had married by wave 6 (right plots). For afternoons and evenings, time spent with friends is expressed as the percentage of respondents who reported spending more than three afternoons or evenings per week with friends. Weekend time (which was measured using a different metric) is expressed as the percentage of respondents who said that they spend "a great deal" or "quite a bit" of their weekend time with friends.

If marriage does in fact affect time spent with peers, respondents who were unmarried at both waves should exhibit little decline in time spent with friends across the two waves, whereas those who married between the waves should show a substantial drop. Figure 5.6 shows that this is precisely the case. Regardless of the time in question (evening, afternoon, or weekend), respondents who remained unmarried at both waves experienced no decline (in fact, small increases) in time spent with friends. By contrast, those who had married by wave 6 display very large, statistically significant drops in time spent with friends, ranging from 43 to 80 percent. This pattern remains unaltered even after controlling for age at marriage (not shown).

After illustrating how marriage affects peer relations, I presented additional longitudinal and cross-sectional evidence indicating that changes in peer relations account for the effect of marriage on desistance. Specifically, when measures of peer influence were held constant, the effect of marriage on delinquency was largely erased. For many individuals, it seems, marriage marks a transition from heavy peer involvement to a preoccupation with one's spouse and family of procreation. For those with a history of crime or delinquency, that transition is likely to reduce interaction with former friends and accomplices and thereby reduce the opportunities as well as the motivation to engage in crime. In words that Sutherland might have chosen, marriage appears to discourage crime by severing or weakening former criminal associations.

Age, Peers, and Identity

As we have seen, there are sound reasons to suspect that the age distribution of crime is attributable to changing peer relations, and that the gradual weakening of peer influence in late adolescence and early adulthood is a consequence of life-course events – marriage, full-time employment, and other passages to adulthood – that disrupt or sever peer ties. What remains uncertain today, however, is whether declining peer influence in early adulthood stems not only from external events like employment and marriage, but also from *internal* psychological/ developmental processes that are independent of these events and that unfold according to their own rules.

Some developmental psychologists argue that as adolescents acquire greater self-awareness and a stronger, more stable sense of identity, they rely less on peers to define themselves and to provide entertainment or excitement in their leisure time. Csikszentmihalyi and Larson (1984: 275), for example, state that "many older adolescents

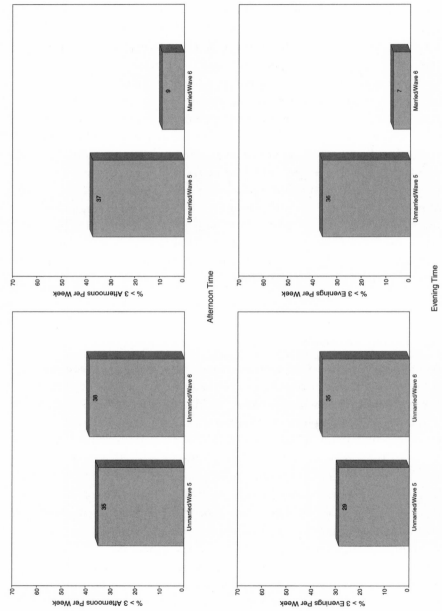

Figure 5.6. Changes in time spent with friends among those who married between waves 5 and 6 (right) and those who remained unmarried (left).

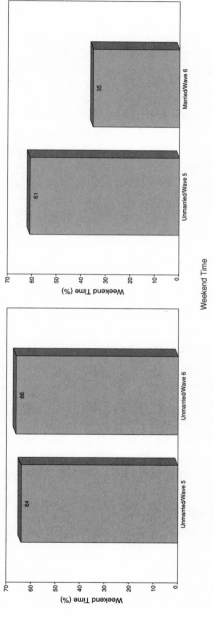

Figure 5.6. (continued)

seem to have developed a strong enough identity to resist the pressure of friends." They go on to quote (1984: 275) one of their subjects on this point:

> Two years ago if they had bothered me I wouldn't have told them to leave me alone; now if they bug me I tell them to go somewhere.... I'd rather be alone than with my friends, cause they always want you to do things and I'd rather do what I want to do.

Thus, while life-course transitions like marriage and full-time work may drive some young people from the company of their peers, others may display greater detachment solely as a consequence of increasing psychological and emotional autonomy. Separating these superficially similar but fundamentally distinct processes in the lives of real individuals is likely to prove a difficult task.

PARENTS, PEERS, AND DELINQUENCY

Whatever one might think about the strength of peer influence in the lives of adolescents, there is no denying that there is another powerful influence at work in their lives as well: the family. In the United States, adolescents live their daily lives in two social worlds with two different masters. At school and in certain activities outside the school, they observe and participate in the culture of their peers, a culture with its own rules of dress, music, speech, and behavior, and an emphasis on popularity, physical attractiveness, and athletic success (Coleman, 1961; Conger and Petersen, 1984). From this culture they move regularly to the environment of home and family, an environment that may complement or clash with that of school and peers. The transitions between these two worlds are frequent – occurring many times each week – and often abrupt.

Criminologists have for decades recognized the importance of both family and peers in the production of delinquency, but these two domains are commonly analyzed in isolation. Proponents of differential association, for example, conventionally point to peer influences while discounting or ignoring the family, whereas control theorists and others concerned with the family do precisely the opposite. This division makes for a certain intellectual neatness and theoretical contrast, but it seems wholly unrealistic. It is difficult to believe, after all, that adolescents leave the influence of their friends entirely behind when they enter the front door at home, or that parental influence extends no further than the mailbox.

One way to conceptually integrate peer and parental influence is to place them within a larger, sequential life-course paradigm, as witness this observation (1995: 279) by Farrington and West:

> [F]rom birth, children are under the influence of the parents, who generally discourage offending. However, during their teenage years, children gradually break away from the control of their parents and become influenced by their peers, who encourage offending in many cases. After age 20, offending declines as peer influence gives way to family influence again, but this time originating in spouses rather than parents.

During the years of adolescence, however, family and peers are commonly viewed as *competitors* in the lives of adolescents, and this approach seems to be justified when it comes to delinquency. Under the logic of differential association theory (Sutherland, 1947) and control theory (Hirschi, 1969), for example, peers are regarded as potential *instigators* of delinquency, and parents as potential *barriers* to delinquency. This formulation appears to be justified not only on theoretical grounds, but for empirical reasons as well. Parents, it seems, exhibit almost universal disapproval of delinquent behavior, and even parents who themselves violate the law evidently do not condone or encourage such behavior among their children (Hirschi, 1969; Jensen, 1972; Jensen and Brownfield, 1983; Wilson and Herrnstein, 1985; Warr, 1993b). By contrast, peer culture provides a host of delinquent models for adolescents and a much more tolerant environment when it comes to delinquency (e.g., Hagan, 1991; Warr, 1993a).

If parents and peers are viewed as potential adversaries or competitors in the lives of adolescents, a question naturally emerges: Is parental influence capable of counteracting peer influence? Put another way, can the motivation toward delinquency generated by one social environment (peer culture) be neutralized by another (the family)? Assuming that the answer is yes, what is the mechanism or process by which this occurs?

There are at least three ways in which parental influence may counteract that of peers in the everyday lives of adolescents. Two of these processes can be described as access barriers, meaning that they restrict adolescents' exposure to or access to delinquent peers. The first mechanism appears in the work of Sutherland (1947) and Hirschi (1969), both of whom noted the importance of *time* in the genesis of delinquency. Put simply, parents who spend time with their children may reduce the likelihood of delinquent behavior, either by reducing opportunities for delinquency (time spent with parents is time spent away from delinquent peers) or by maximizing their effect as positive (law-abiding) role models. In Hirschi's (1969: 88) words, "The child attached to his parents may be less likely to get into situations in which delinquent acts are possible, simply because he spends more of his time in their presence." Because adolescents spend many of their waking hours away from parents at school, the ability of parents to control exposure to delinquent peers is limited. But what parents do during their children's time *away* from school may nonetheless be pivotally important when it comes to delinquency.

A second mechanism speaks not to the availability of time for delinquent friends, but rather to the formation of delinquent friendships themselves. That is, adolescents who are strongly attached to their parents may be less prone than others to acquire delinquent friends and hence less motivated to engage in delinquency. This may occur because these adolescents wittingly or unwittingly seek out nondelinquent peers to avoid parental disapproval, or, alternatively, because the parents of these adolescents actively regulate the friendships of their offspring to screen out undesirable companions (e.g., Dishion, Patterson, and Griesler, 1994). In either case, the argument is that attachment to parents and having delinquent friends are negatively associated with one another.

Both of the preceding mechanisms presuppose that parental influence operates by preventing or reducing exposure to delinquent peers. By the mid-teens, however, the majority of American adolescents are likely to have at least some delinquent friends (Warr, 1993a), either because they are unavoidable, tolerable, or outright desirable. In the inner city, for example, exposure to delinquent peers is virtually inevitable as children from "decent" families and "street" families mingle in the same neighborhoods (Anderson, 1999).

It is when adolescents are directly exposed to delinquent friends that parental influence is subjected to its most stringent test. Although peer influence appears to be quite strong, there are nevertheless reasons to suppose that parental influence may withstand direct competition from peers under some circumstances. Among adolescents with strong bonds to their parents, the potential loss of parental approval or parental affection may be sufficient to deter delinquency even when pressure from peers is strong. Similarly, adolescents who are close to their parents may be more likely than others to internalize and act on their parents' moral inhibitions against delinquency, providing an obstacle or barrier to peer influence. The larger point is that parents may be "psychologically present" (to use Hirschi's [1969: 88] phrase) even when adolescents are in the company of delinquent peers or otherwise under their influence.

Sifting through these possibilities in search of the truth is a formidable task, but the history of research in this area offers grounds for optimism. Amid the scores of studies that have examined parents and peers, there is strong and consistent evidence of an inverse relation between attachment to parents and having delinquent friends. Kids who are close to their parents, in other words, are less likely to report having delinquent friends than those who are not. The empirical evidence for this position is so extensive that many investigators today treat attachment to parents as a direct cause of delinquent associations in statistical and/or conceptual models of delinquency (e.g., Hirschi, 1969; Devereux, 1970; Jensen, 1972; Matsueda, 1982; Elliott, Huizinga, and Ageton, 1985; Patterson and Dishion, 1985; Marcos, Bahr, and Johnson, 1986; Massey and Krohn, 1986; Fuligni and Eccles, 1993; Warr, 1993b; Simons et al., 1994; Fergusson and Horwood, 1999).

So compelling is the evidence on this matter that some investigators (e.g., Elliott, Huizinga, and Ageton, 1985) see it as reason to integrate Hirschi's (1969) famous control theory of delinquency with peer-oriented theories like differential association. A key element of

Hirschi's theory is the relation between children and their parents; children with weak attachment or bonds to their parents, Hirschi argued, are most likely to engage in crime. Proponents of integrated theories agree, but argue that this occurs because children with weak bonds to their parents are precisely those who are most likely to acquire delinquent friends. If differential association and control theory are united through this common element, then peer influence can be viewed as the proximate cause of delinquency in a longer causal chain in which "parents have an indirect influence on their children's deviance through the kinds of peers with whom the children affiliate" (Kandel, 1996: 292). There is in fact substantial evidence for this integrated theory, and some of its advocates (see especially Elliott, Huizinga, and Ageton, 1985; Thornberry, 1987) regard it as the single best empirically substantiated theory of crime that can be offered by modern criminology.

The Contest between Parents and Peers

Although attachment to parents and delinquent peers are strongly and negatively associated, the association is not perfect, and some adolescents who are attached to their parents will nevertheless have delinquent friends (see Jensen, 1972; Warr, 1993a, 1993b; Anderson, 1999). There is reason to believe that parental attachment does *not* reduce the impact of delinquent peers *among adolescents who are already exposed to such peers* (see Warr, 1993b). Although attachment to parents seems to inhibit the initial development of delinquent friendships, it apparently does little to reduce delinquency among those who have acquired delinquent friends.

Once adolescents have acquired delinquent peers, is the battle between family and peers lost? Or is the family capable of counteracting peer influence? Some clear and rather surprising evidence on this question can be found in a study by the author (Warr, 1993b) that examined the interaction between *time* spent with the family and time spent with delinquent peers in determining delinquent behavior. In that study, data from the National Youth Survey were used to conduct analyses of covariance for six delinquent offenses, with delinquent friends as the covariate and family time represented by a set of dummy variables. The analysis disclosed that the impact of delinquent friends was weakest among adolescents who spent much of their weekend time with their families. In the case of the two most serious offenses examined (burglary and grand larceny), the effect of delinquent friends *was entirely offset by weekend time.* That is, the slope was effectively zero (i.e., not statistically different from zero) among those who spent the most time with their families. In the remaining cases, the effect of friends was significantly reduced, though not entirely eliminated, by weekend time, and the investigation uncovered similar but less powerful effects of afternoon and evening time. Although there were not enough forms of delinquency for a full evaluation, it appears that family time is a potent factor in inhibiting more serious forms of delinquent behavior.

The results of this research suggest that *time* spent with the family can counteract and even overcome peer influence, but *attachment* to parents is evidently insufficient to do so. Why? To reiterate my own conclusion:

> If time spent with parents is capable of counterbalancing peer influence, why is the same not true for attachment to parents? The reason, I suspect, is that the immediate pressure of peers on adolescents is so great that peer-induced pressures to violate the law can be overcome only by avoiding the company of delinquent peers altogether. This may be achieved either by inhibiting the formation of delinquent friendships in the first place (as attachment to parents seems to do) or by reducing the time that adolescents spend with their delinquent friends. When adolescents are away from their parents and amid their peers, after all, the moral inhibitions of parents or the potential loss of parental approval may seem like distant concerns, especially when the possibility of discovery appears to be remote. It may be too strong to say that "out of sight is out of mind" when it comes to parents, but that interpretation is not inconsistent with these findings. Still, it would be a mistake to discount the importance of parental attachment as an *indirect* cause of delinquency, in view of its apparent effect on friendship selection. (Warr, 1993b: 259)

To proponents of peer influence, the most surprising aspect of this research may be the notion that peer influence can be prevented or reduced at all. As advocates of differential association and other peer-oriented theories are quick to point out, no variable is more strongly correlated with delinquency than the number of delinquent friends an adolescent has, nor has any correlation been more frequently demonstrated in the delinquency literature. However, in the contest between parents and peers, peers are not always the winners, it seems, nor is their influence ineluctable. In view of the strength normally attributed to peer influence, this is no minor observation.

These findings also raise serious questions about the emphasis on "quality time" so prevalent in the family literature today. Although "quality time" is surely something to be desired, the *quantity* of time spent with the family, it seems, is not irrelevant. Contemporary arguments notwithstanding, small amounts of quality time may not be enough to offset the criminogenic aspects of peer culture to which adolescents are commonly exposed. In an era when family time is at a premium and family structure has been shaken, the notion of the family as an effective obstacle to delinquency may be difficult to accept. But if the family is capable of counteracting one of the strongest influences on American adolescents, it cannot easily be dismissed.

GENDER AND DELINQUENCY

Let us now look at one final controversy in criminology: the relation between gender and delinquent conduct.

Gender is one of the strongest and most frequently documented correlates of delinquent behavior. Males commit more offenses than females at every age, within all racial and ethnic groups examined to date, and for all but a handful of offense types that are peculiarly female (Wilson and Herrnstein, 1985; Steffensmeier and Allan, 1995). Unlike some putative features of delinquency that are method-dependent (e.g., social class differences), sex differences in delinquency are independently corroborated by self-report, victimization, and police data, and they appear to hold cross-culturally as well as historically

(Hindelang, 1979; Hindelang, Hirschi, and Weis, 1979; Wilson and Herrnstein, 1985; Steffensmeier and Allan, 1995). So tenacious are sex differences in delinquency, in fact, that it is difficult to argue with Wilson and Herrnstein's conclusion (1985: 104) that "gender demands attention in the search for the origins of crime."

Explanations of gender differences in offending have been promulgated at least since the time of Lombroso, who asserted that the female criminal is "of less typical aspect than the male because she is less essentially criminal" (Lombroso and Ferrero, 1958 [1895]: 111). Lombroso's viewpoint notwithstanding, efforts to explain the gender/crime relation have not fared well, and some sharp philosophical and methodological differences have arisen as to how investigators ought to proceed. Some analysts argue that conventional theories of delinquency were largely designed to explain male delinquency and that separate theories are required to account for male and female delinquency. Smith and Paternoster (1987: 142), however, strongly warn against premature rejection of existing theories: "Since most empirical tests of deviance theories have been conducted with male samples, the applicability of these theories to females is largely unknown. Moreover, the fact that most theories of deviance were constructed to account for male deviance does not mean that they *cannot* account for female deviance."

Rather than postulating separate etiological theories for males and females, Smith and Paternoster (1987) join a number of investigators (cf. Simons, Miller, and Aigner, 1980) in suggesting that males and females differ in their rates of delinquency because they are *differentially exposed* to the *same* criminogenic conditions. In a close variant of this position, other investigators (e.g., Johnson, 1979) have suggested that males and females are differentially *affected* by exposure to the same criminogenic conditions. If such arguments are correct, then it is pointless to construct entirely separate theories to explain the delinquent behavior of males and females.

One traditional theory of delinquency that holds promise for a unified explanation of gender differences in offending is Sutherland's (1947) theory of differential association, which argues that delinquency is learned largely in intimate social groups through face-to-face interaction. Several studies suggest that differential association may be a critical factor in explaining gender differences in delinquency. Using self-report data from a sample of Iowa teenagers, Simons, Miller, and Aigner (1980) found that males and females experienced substantially different levels of exposure to delinquent peer attitudes in their everyday lives. "Males were much more likely than females to have friends who were supportive of delinquent behavior" (1980: 51). But although these investigators were able to establish sex-linked differences in exposure to delinquent friends, they did not isolate and quantify the effect of such exposure on sex-specific rates of delinquency.

Other studies illustrate the variant approach described earlier. Johnson (1979) tested an integrated model of delinquency containing family, school, socioeconomic, deterrence, and peer variables. Both among males and among females, the effect of delinquent associates outweighed all other variables in the model. But the effect of delinquent peers on self-reported delinquency was substantially stronger among males than among females. Smith and Paternoster (1987) examined the ability of strain theory, differential association, control theory, and deterrence theory to explain sex differences in adolescent marijuana use. They too found that association with deviant peers had the largest effect on marijuana use among both males and females, but the effect was once again stronger for males than for females. Despite the strikingly similar findings of these two studies, not all investigators have obtained similar results (see Smith and Paternoster, 1987). Many, however, have failed to employ appropriate interaction terms or tests of significance in making gender comparisons, or have used widely divergent measures of peer influence.

In a novel approach to explaining gender differences in offending, Mears, Ploeger, and Warr (1998) employed Sutherland's theory of differential association as well as Gilligan's (1982) theory of moral development. Gilligan argued that moral development in females is guided by the primacy of human relationships and by an overriding obligation to care for and *to avoid harming* others. This other-oriented quality of female moral development, she added, contrasts sharply with the moral socialization of males. If the moral imperative of women is "an injunction to care" (1982: 100), Gilligan argued, men tend to construe morality in more utilitarian terms, that is, as a set of mutually acknowledged rights that protect them from *interference* from others. Thus the driving principle of male morality is not responsibility to others, but the freedom to pursue self-interest. These gender-linked differences in socialization described by Gilligan imply that females will be more reluctant than males to engage in conduct that harms others, including criminal conduct.

Drawing on Sutherland and Gilligan, Mears, Ploeger, and Warr (1998) argued that gender differences in delinquent behavior may occur because males and females differ in their exposure to delinquent peers, and because males and females are differentially *affected* by exposure to delinquent peers. In the latter case, they argued, moral inhibitions act as a barrier among females, making them less susceptible than males to the influence of delinquent peers.

Using data from the National Youth Survey, Mears, Ploeger, and Warr showed that males are approximately 1.5 to 2.5 times (depending on the offense) more likely than females to have friends who engage in illegal conduct. But this fact alone, they determined, could not fully explain sex differences in offending. The authors also found that females reported significantly greater moral disapproval of every offense measured in the survey. But this fact could not, by itself, explain the sex differences in delinquency that they observed. Instead, the critical mechanism generating sex differences in offending, they concluded, was the impact of moral inhibitions in *blocking the influence of delinquent peers*. Among both males and females, they found, strong moral inhibitions acted as a barrier to peer influence. But that barrier was much stronger among females than among males. By "insulating" females from peer influence, strong moral inhibitions acted to discourage delinquency even among those females who had many delinquent friends.

SUMMARY

The purpose of this chapter has been to demonstrate the viability of peer influence as an answer to some of the most enduring questions about delinquent behavior. At the least, the evidence has shown that peer influence is a serious contender in explaining certain fundamental features of delinquency, some of which have remained unresolved since the field of criminology was founded more than a century ago. What is perhaps most encouraging is the possibility that a single explanation may be capable of simultaneously explaining several of those features, a prospect that holds out hope for the sort of parsimony and simplicity rarely seen in the social sciences. As noted earlier, that explanation draws on familiar and well-documented features of adolescence, features that are readily observable by anyone who takes but a few minutes to watch the younger members of our society.

CHAPTER SIX

Conclusion

This book has been an effort to organize and evaluate the evidence concerning peer influence and criminal behavior. That delinquent behavior is predominantly group behavior is beyond dispute. That having delinquent friends is associated with delinquent behavior is equally indisputable. That these facts have any etiological significance when it comes to delinquent behavior, however, *is* disputable.

Some criminologists, as we have seen, dismiss these facts with scarcely a pause, either because they appear to be inconsequential, contradict a preferred theory, or can be readily explained away. In one of the more influential books in criminology in recent years, for example, Gottfredson and Hirschi (1990) utterly rejected the notion of peer influence and instead attributed criminal behavior to an absence of self-control. Gottfredson and Hirschi's distaste for peer explanations seems odd, however, when one considers that one of the principal ways by which groups seem to affect individuals is precisely by *dissolving their self-control* (see Chapter 4). The authors also make much of the similarities between criminal events and accidents – both ostensible consequences of low self-control. Yet among adolescents, the probability of a fatal motor vehicle accident increases in direct proportion to the number of adolescents in the vehicle (Chen et al., 2000).

Like a gorilla in the living room, the social nature of crime seems to push some investigators to extraordinary lengths in their efforts to ignore it. To those who approach the topic of crime from a disinterested position, however, it is difficult to understand how investigators could overlook one of its most irrepressible features, even if they have doubts about its ultimate significance. The social nature of crime, after all, is one of its most lawlike features, and it is no different in this way from the age and sex-linked differences in crime that have so fascinated criminologists. In addition, there are a number of plausible theories of peer influence, and variability in peer relations, as we have seen in the previous chapter, is potentially capable of explaining some of the essential facts of criminal behavior.

One reason that peer explanations of delinquency remain so contentious and unsettled, I believe, is that the evidence in favor of them remains largely indirect. By that I mean to say that existing evidence on peer influence is largely correlational and often highly inferential, facts that leave room for legitimate questions about causal direction, selection effects, and other alternative explanations. As the Cairns (1994: 100) have noted, "It is a minor irony that the richness of theoretical speculations about peer groups and their influence has been matched by the poverty of empirical data available."

Although research on peers clearly suggests the existence of some kind of peer influence, investigators have yet to pinpoint or even narrow the number of possible mechanisms by which such influence operates. Were they to do so, even in a limited way, much of the conventional skepticism about peer influence might well evaporate. The truth, however, is that despite strong and persistent evidence of peer influence in the etiology of delinquency, the exact mechanism(s) by which peers "transmit" or encourage delinquent behavior among one another remains a mystery.

The task of identifying such mechanisms is admittedly daunting, for there are some seemingly insurmountable methodological problems confronting those who choose to study peer influence. Nearly all research on peer influence and delinquency, for example, has relied on survey methods; yet those methods are inherently limited for such purposes. Conventional survey methods capture delinquent events after the fact (often long after the fact), through the clouded lens of memory, and with little ability to accurately place those events in time or in the social context in which they occurred. Adolescents can change friends numerous times between the occurrence of a delinquent event and a survey measurement of that event, and their life circumstances may have changed as well. Experimental methods, despite their potential advantages with regard to causal certainty, are difficult to apply to group behavior and criminal conduct in ways that do not compromise their external validity, and they often raise ethical concerns.

One fresh way to approach the matter is to borrow from the life-course perspective, which has come to be adopted in many fields, including criminology. As I noted earlier, a life-course approach shifts the units of analysis from individuals to periods or phases within individuals' lives, facilitating both intra- and interindividual comparisons. A serious problem with conventional life-course approaches, however, is that they often focus exclusive attention on major life-course transitions/phases like marriage, employment, parenthood, and college attendance. As important as these events are, an approach as coarse as this is likely to miss finer, more short-lived phenomena like adolescent friendships (which constantly change – see Cairns and Cairns, 1994) and even most criminal careers, which tend to be short (Steffensmeier and Allan, 1995).

In view of this problem, a preferable strategy for studying peer influence is to employ what could be called a *micro-life-course* perspective. Under this approach, changes during the life course remain the focus of attention, but the resolution shifts from months or years to days, weeks, or even hours. The most obvious advantage of this approach is the ability to measure brief events – transitory friendships, delinquent episodes – shortly after they occur, or even as they take place. There are other benefits as well. One of the principal advantages of the experimental method with respect to causal inference is its repeatability. The ability to produce an outcome consistently and reliably increases one's confidence that the causal mechanism has been effectively isolated. Given the brevity of many adolescent friendships, the formation/dissolution of peer ties during adolescence is likely to be sufficiently frequent to enable repeated tests of peer influence within the biographies of individuals, a strategy that offers the advantages of case control along with the potential to control for major life-course transitions within and across individuals.

Figure 6.1 shows how one might examine peer influences for a single individual using the micro-life-course approach. Once detailed data on peer contacts have been gathered (see Figure 6.1), information on the timing of those contacts (e.g., time since last contact, density and duration of contacts, overlap among contacts with different peers) can be integrated with information on each peer (emotional closeness, delinquent history, age, propinquity, socioeconomic status) to predict the subject's behavior at any point in time. Cumulative or lagged effects could be estimated, and data on the onset and cessation of friendships could potentially yield important evidence concerning the causal direction between delinquent behavior and peer associations. In addition, extended longitudinal data of this kind would permit investigators to assess (or control for) other life-course changes that are confounded with peer relations over time (e.g., changes in employment and in family conditions).

Critics might well ask: Even if this sort of design is desirable, how could it be implemented? One of my mentors – the late Maynard Erickson – used to argue to me that the only way to properly and effectively measure the group features of delinquency was through the use of daily diaries maintained by subjects (see also Emler and Reicher, 1995). Only through that method, he believed, could one keep account of the everchanging sociometry of delinquent groups and the fleeting nature of peer influence. The diary method might seem awkward and untenable, but diaries have been used to good effect to measure phenomena like the division of labor in family households (who does the cooking and washing, who takes care of the kids?). Another possibility is the ingenious and fruitful method employed by Csikszentmihalyi and Larson (1984), who gave beepers to teenagers and contacted them at random intervals to find out what they were doing.

The micro-life-course method may enable us to draw some strong conclusions about the existence and strength of peer influence and may help to resolve questions about the timing and causal direction of such influence. Less likely, however, is the possibility that it will tell

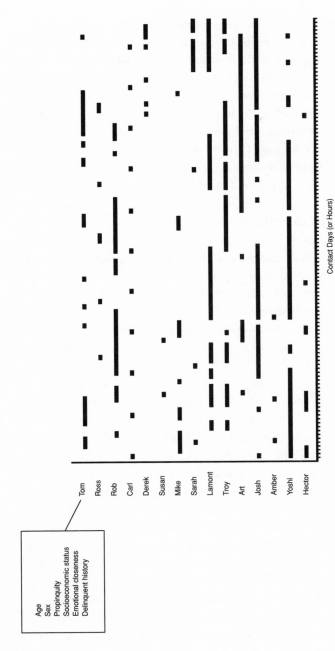

Figure 6.1. Illustration of the micro-life-course approach.

us exactly how such influence operates. In that matter, there is simply no substitute for systematically and methodically testing the possibilities described in Chapter 4. Nevertheless, it makes more sense to determine *whether* peer influence can be reliably demonstrated before investing the resources required to determine *how* it works. Whatever strategy is ultimately chosen, however, it is essential to examine both short-term and long-term patterns of peer relations over the life course – what might be called "peer careers" – if the goal is to illuminate the process of peer influence.

PEERS AND PUBLIC POLICY

Let us assume for the moment that delinquent conduct among adolescents is in fact a consequence of peer influence in one form or another. If so, then what practical implications does this have for controlling or reducing delinquency? Theories about the causes of crime are intrinsically interesting to many people, of course, but in a society beset by the hard realities of crime, a theory of crime causation ought to be something more than an intellectual exercise or mere armchair speculation. It should be pressed to offer some means to prevent or control crime in the real world.

Controlling crime, of course, does not necessarily require an understanding of its causes; prisons and the death penalty are proof enough of that. But just as a physician would rather prevent a disease than attempt to cure it after it is established (many diseases are incurable once under way), stopping crime *before* it happens by understanding and altering its causes is surely the most defensible and profitable course of action. Unfortunately, because it is an intrinsically long-term strategy, prevention is a difficult policy to sell to a skeptical and frightened public or to politicians interested only in the short term. Worse still, the very evidence that prevention is working is the fact that *nothing happens*. Demonstrating that something did not happen today because of strategies that were adopted years ago is, both empirically and politically, a difficult task. American culture, it would seem, has neither the patience nor the foresight to implement and monitor serious prevention programs.

Unlike some etiological theories in criminology, theories that emphasize peer influence have clear and practical implications for preventing or reducing crime. It is difficult to imagine a theory of crime, for example, that has more direct and unambiguous policy implications than Sutherland's theory of differential association. To reduce the probability that an individual will engage in criminal conduct, one must limit or control his or her exposure to delinquent associates. Many policies and programs designed to reduce crime do in fact draw on this principle, if not always consciously or carefully. For example, after-school and summertime recreational programs for adolescents often are designed to provide an alternative to hanging out with the "wrong crowd." Parents frequently encourage their children to participate in sports, scouting, or church activities on the grounds that their children will make friends with "good kids." Parents are themselves often urged to supervise their children closely and to pay special attention to those with whom they spend their time.

Do such programs or policies work? Not necessarily, though for reasons that are not always obvious. For example, parents of high school students sometimes encourage their children to get jobs in order to fill their time and keep them away from the wrong kinds of kids. As noted earlier, however, employment is *positively* correlated with delinquency among adolescents, and one of the reasons seems to be that adolescents often work in settings where they associate with many of their age-peers and have little or no adult supervision (Ploeger, 1997). In a similar way, keeping a child away from other children only to put him or her in front of a television set bursting with violent programs may not have the intended effect.

Still, there are reasons to believe that regulating exposure to peers is an effective strategy for delinquency prevention. As we saw earlier, Warr (1993b) found that adolescents who reported spending much of their time each week with the family had low rates of delinquency *even when they had delinquent friends*. This finding strongly suggests that the family is ultimately capable of counteracting or overcoming peer influence. This may be true merely because spending time with the family limits opportunities to engage in delinquency, but the effect remains the same. In addition, research consistently indicates (see Warr, 1993b) that adolescents who are close to their parents are less likely to report having any delinquent friends in the first place. This may occur because their parents monitor their friendships or because such children do not want to displease their parents, but in either case the point is that parents can reduce the chances that their children will have delinquent friends by remaining emotionally close to their children. Where this proves difficult or impossible to achieve, prohibiting or minimizing contact with delinquent friends ought to be an effective means of delinquency control. At the same time, however, parents who are *overly* restrictive can push their children toward delinquent peers and exacerbate the very problem they seek to avoid (Fuligni and Eccles, 1993).

The fundamental dilemma facing parents, of course, is that while peer associations carry the risk of delinquency, acquiring friends and achieving intimacy with age-mates is an essential and healthy part of adolescence, and depriving kids of time with their friends may have serious long-term consequences. In addition, spotting "bad" kids among one's children's friends is not always an easy task, and even hanging out with "good" kids may on occasion lead to inappropriate conduct.

Many intelligent parents attempt to keep a close eye on their children's associations by maintaining contacts with the parents of their children's friends. That is probably a wise course of action, but the fact is that none of the parents of an adolescent group may know what goes on in that group during unsupervised times. In the end, the only persons who are in a position to know are the adolescents themselves, and that argues strongly for maintaining trust and open lines of communication with one's children, even to the point of foregoing or limiting punishment at times in return for a child's honesty. For many parents, achieving such a degree of communication may seem hopelessly difficult and even unrealizable, but the alternative is to turn over the task of socializing one's own children to others, others who may have no stake in the outcome.

PENDING QUESTIONS

Through the course of this book I have raised many questions about peer influence, most having to do with its nature or with issues of evidence. There remain a number of important empirical questions about peer influence, however, that deserve careful consideration as topics for further research.

Old Friends

Most studies of peer influence concentrate on the relations among adolescents and their current friends, a reasonable place to begin investigation. But adolescents' behavior at any particular time may be affected by those they have known in the past as well as by those who share their present. Indeed, it was precisely such a possibility that led Sutherland to stipulate the "priority" of relationships as one of the key elements of his theory of differential association. Under Sutherland's conceptualization, relationships at earlier ages are allegedly more consequential in shaping later behavior than more recent relationships. Sutherland offered no explicit rationale for this point of view, but it seemed to rest on an assumption that individuals are more impressionable in their younger, formative years.

As noted earlier, however, adolescents' behavior is more strongly correlated with the behavior of their current friends than with that of prior friends, and the similarity between adolescents' present behavior and the behavior of friends at earlier ages declines steadily as the interval between the two increases (Warr, 1993a). Consequently, adolescents seem to be most strongly influenced by their immediate friends, and the impact of previous relationships evidently recedes fairly quickly. This phenomenon appears to support situational (or at least short-term) explanations of peer influence, under which behavior depends on whom one is with *now*. It also accords with social learning theory in the sense that behavior that is no longer reinforced (as might happen when one changes friends) is eventually extinguished.

At a practical level, the apparent decay in peer influence over time means that investigators must pay close attention to the temporal lags specified in longitudinal models of peer influence. For example, Matsueda and Anderson (1998) report smaller peer effects than those obtained in many studies of peer influence, but they employed lag times that were considerably longer than those found in most investigations. Their study examined waves 1, 3, and 5 of the National Youth Survey, meaning that subjects' and friends' behaviors were separated by a period of up to several years. In fact, even self-report studies that purportedly rely on contemporaneous measures of subject and peer behavior often use reference periods (the period about which questions are asked) of a full year, permitting large potential gaps between these two variables. Because the life span of adolescent friendships is often measured in weeks or months (e.g., Cairns and Cairns, 1994), even "contemporaneous" measures of this kind can result in significant measurement error and potentially erroneous conclusions. The micro-life-course approach advocated earlier resolves such problems by minimizing gaps in the chain of observations.

Apart from attending to temporal lags, the crucial issue confronting investigators is how to assess the effect, if any, of prior friends. Although the effects of former friends may recede quickly, they may not disappear altogether, and their cumulative effect may not be trivial. And although friends come and go rapidly during adolescence, some friendships are of much greater duration than others, and there is reason to believe that longer friendships have longer-lasting consequences (Warr, 1993a). Then, too, one of the lessons learned from research on peer rejection (e.g., Parker and Asher, 1987) seems to be that peer relations (or at least this form of peer relations) can have measurable effects long after they have ceased. Finally, the choice of friends at any one time (that is, the pool of available associates) may be influenced or constrained by earlier choices, a possibility that is envisioned by labeling theory. In fact, it seems that delinquent friends are often "sticky friends"; once acquired, they are not easily lost (Warr, 1993a).

The larger point is that investigators must pay careful attention to the *histories* of peer relations among their subjects, histories that may differ substantially even for those adolescents who have similar *current* friendship patterns.

Age and Co-offending

Earlier, I noted that the propensity to commit crime with others declines with age. The larger delinquent groups of early adolescence are replaced by the triads and dyads of middle and late adolescence and, eventually, by predominantly solitary offending in the early twenties (Reiss, 1986; Hood and Sparks, 1970; Reiss and Farrington, 1991). This seemingly straightforward process, however, is complicated by the age distribution of crime itself; recall that age-specific rates of offending peak in the middle to late teens for most offenses. Taken together, these two phenomena – the age distribution of *crime* and the age distribution of *co-offending* – mean that the transition to lone offending occurs at the same time that most offenders are abandoning crime. The interaction between these two processes is not well understood, and it may be complex. To complicate matters even further, buried within the general age distributions of offending and co-offending may lie smaller, specialized populations with age distributions that are distinct from, and are masked by, the general population.

To illustrate these possibilities, consider a phenomenon that might be called *selective desistance*. Imagine a small subset of offenders who require no social support of any kind for their criminal activity, who are primarily or exclusively lone offenders, and who persist in crime long after the age at which most offenders have desisted (i.e., well into adulthood). Now imagine a much larger group of "ordinary" offenders who require co-offenders for most or all of their delinquent behavior and who follow the general age distribution of offending. As these ordinary offenders increasingly desist from crime in late adolescence and early adulthood, those offenders who remain active will increasingly be composed of persons from the first category. Taken as a whole, the combined age distributions of these two groups would resemble the familiar age distribution of crime itself (see Chapter 5), with offending dropping sharply in late adolescence and early adulthood, and with a small minority of offenders who persist into later life. Yet what would at first appear to be a single unitary process would actually, under this scenario, be the unfolding of two quite different processes.

This hypothetical situation corresponds, at least generally, to what Moffitt (1993) had in mind when she posited the existence of "life-course-persistent" offenders and "adolescence-limited" offenders. The former, she argued, suffer from a neurophysiological deficit that is present from an early age and that contributes to criminality throughout life. The latter, much larger group consists of adolescents who are reacting to the temporary "maturity gap" between the privileges of young people and those of adults. Whether this particular formulation is correct or not, recent research has suggested that there may in fact be discernible subgroups of offenders with distinctly different age trajectories (D'Unger et al., 1998). The key to explaining such trajectories may lie in examining not only the offending histories of each group but their *co*-offending histories as well.

To date, few criminologists have paid much attention to the decline in group offending that occurs with age, perhaps because the kind of data required to examine it – protracted longitudinal data on group offending – is quite scarce (for an exception, see Reiss and Farrington, 1991). This state of affairs is most unfortunate, because if the group nature of delinquency does have any etiological significance, then any event or process that diminishes group offending deserves serious attention.

Heterogeneity of Motivation in Groups

Most conventional theories of delinquency focus on individuals rather than groups, and pay no theoretical attention to the group nature of delinquency. Consequently, they seem to portray delinquent groups as mere aggregates of like-minded or similarly motivated individuals. As I have frequently noted in this book, however, one cannot simply assume that all members of delinquent groups are equally motivated or inclined to break the law on any particular occasion, and there are grounds for suspecting otherwise.

Reiss (1986; see also Warr, 1996) distinguished between "instigators" and "joiners" in delinquent groups in an effort to capture apparent differences in intent and motivation, but even that distinction probably fails to adequately reflect the full range of motivation within many groups (not to mention differences in the same group from one occasion to the next). In criminal law, which must attempt to anticipate and codify the sometimes complex relations among co-offenders, various degrees of individual or joint motivation among offenders are conventionally recognized. Under the word "accomplice," for example, *Black's Law Dictionary* (1968: 33) distinguishes between persons who share "common intent" and those who contribute only through their "presence, acquiescence, or silence." As one type of *particeps criminis* (participant in crime), an *abettor* (from the French word meaning to bait an animal) is one who "commands, advises, instigates, or encourages another to commit a crime" (1968: 17). By contrast, one who merely "aids" a crime lacks criminal intent and knowledge of the wrongful purpose of the perpetrator (1968: 17). Still another *particeps criminis* is an *accessory before the fact,* or "one who, being absent at the time a crime is committed, yet assists, procures, counsels, incites, induces, encourages, engages, or commands another to commit it" (1968: 29). By convention, some crimes (e.g., treason) do not recognize accessories of any kind; all participants are considered to be principals.

This brief and superficial foray into criminal law is intended merely to illustrate that, in this instance at least, the law is well ahead of social science in imposing conceptual order on human behavior. As for social scientists, why does motivational variability in groups matter? Apart from a duty to accurately describe social behavior, one reason is that different theories of peer influence sometimes imply different degrees of motivation within the group (see Chapter 4). Under some mechanisms of peer influence, one need not assume that each member of the group actually wishes to engage in the conduct in question; to assume otherwise is to "overexplain" the event by overestimating the motivation that led to it, or to mistake the motivations of some group members. As a prelude to testing specific theories of peer influence, it might make sense simply to measure in a systematic way the variability of motivation within (and across) delinquent groups, using methods more refined than the few occasional attempts of the past (e.g., such questions as "Whose idea was it?"). Information of this kind might significantly narrow the field of possibilities when it comes to identifying mechanisms of influence within delinquent groups.

Structural Variation in Peer Associations

Even though it connotes a social process, criminologists typically apply the concept of peer influence to explain individual variability in delinquent behavior, i.e., why one person engages in delinquency while another does not. What researchers often seem to overlook is the possibility that peer interaction may explain some of the larger social-structural correlates of crime – poverty, divorce, illegitimate births – as well, including those variables emphasized by social disorganization theorists and by more recent community approaches to crime (e.g., Bursik and Grasmick, 1993; Sampson and Groves, 1989; see Matsueda and Heimer, 1987, for a rare exception to this rule).

Let us suppose, for example, that children from one-parent households are subject to less parental supervision than children from two-parent households, leaving them with more time on their hands to spend with friends outside the home. The absence of one parent, after all, can seriously handicap the ability of the remaining parent to supervise his or her children, and the situation becomes even more serious if the sole parent must work outside the home to support the family.

If family structure does indeed affect parental supervision and, in turn, exposure to delinquent peers, this fact might explain the frequently observed correlation between crime rates and rates of divorce and other forms of family disruption (desertion, separation). It might also help to explain the correlation between poverty and crime, inasmuch as poor households are disproportionately single-parent (i.e., female-headed) households. For poor families, in addition, money for paid supervision of children is scarce, community activities for youth are often limited or unavailable, and the street or "turf" frequently becomes the hangout of poor youth (e.g., Sullivan, 1989; Anderson, 1999).

Extending the case further, the same logic can be applied to racial and ethnic differentials in offending. African-American families, for example, are far more likely than white families to fall below the poverty line and to be female-headed households, and they are more likely to live in inner city environments where gangs compete for the attention and loyalty of the young and sometimes offer a replacement for the family itself (Anderson, 1999). Parental supervision, of course, may not be the only peer-related variable underlying structural correlates of crime. For example, if low-income parents typically use more harsh or erratic discipline with their children than do high-income parents, then they are more apt to drive their children away from the family and toward their peers (Fuligni and Eccles, 1993).

Among the most important "structural" differences in crime are cross-national differences in crime rates. As we saw in Chapter 2, variation among nations in the role of peers during childhood and adolescence is of such magnitude that it would be remarkable if it did *not* have any impact on crime rates, if only through the availability of co-offenders to young people. Yet efforts to explain differences in crime rates among countries commonly concentrate on variables like economic development, while overlooking peers. As things stand today, even elementary measures of peer influence – time spent with friends or number of friends – are unavailable in any systematic way for most countries of the world, a situation that ought to be intolerable to criminologists. If criminology is ever to become a truly comparative field, it might well begin by examining cross-national differences in peer associations and their relations to crime rates.

Inferring Peer Influence

One of the stronger points of evidence in support of peer influence, as I have observed throughout this book, is the correlation between the behavior of adolescents and that of their friends. Scores of studies conducted over many decades attest to the robustness of this correlation. At the same time, there remain serious questions about what ought and ought not to be construed as evidence of peer influence, and how peer influence should be measured or inferred.

In and of itself, a strong correlation between the behavior of adolescents and that of their friends is of limited value for demonstrating peer influence. Even if we assume that the correlation is indicative of influence rather than selection (homophily), and even if we assume that the correlation is not an artifact of measurement, the correlation itself says nothing about the process or mechanism of influence that gave rise to it, and the number of possibilities is large (see Chapter 4).

And although correlations of this kind are often offered as evidence of peer influence, the comparability and import (i.e., generalizability) of behaviors used in computing such correlations is sometimes open to question. Early studies of peer influence (and a few more recent ones) frequently examined the correlation between respondents' self-reported delinquency and whether or not their friends had ever "had trouble with the police." No attention was given to whether the behaviors of the respondent and his or her friends were similar or comparable. In contemporary research using the National Youth Survey and other comprehensive data sets, respondents are asked about a large variety of specific behaviors that they and their friends may have engaged in. Using data of this kind, many investigators create scales or indices of subjects' and peers' behavior and examine the correlation between the two. With many such indices, however, the precise behaviors of subjects and peers can differ enormously, and there may in fact be no exact overlap in their behavior *at all* (e.g., John sells marijuana while his friend Ronnie steals cars).

When investigators employ such methods, it is often unclear what theory of peer influence they are relying on or attempting to test. For example, the concept of imitation from social learning theory suggests that investigators search for *exact* behavioral parallels among peers, not just general similarities. The same is true if one assumes that peer influence requires the physical presence of peers during delinquent events (i.e., group offending), since subject and friends are presumably participants in the same event(s).

As far as I can determine, investigators who employ broad composite indices of offending seem to be relying on a theory of peer influence that emphasizes some form of attitude transference with very generalized consequences. Having friends who commit *any* kind of delinquency, in other words, supposedly opens the door for adolescents to commit any *other* kind of delinquency. Available evidence, however, consistently fails to support the notion of attitude transference when it comes to peer influence and delinquency (Warr and Stafford, 1991), and there is good reason to believe that compliance with peers does not require shared attitudes at all (see Chapters 1 and 4).

Ultimately, the larger question to be confronted is this: What exactly constitutes evidence of peer influence? If the answer is behavioral similarity, how closely must the behaviors of the parties resemble one another? Criminal conduct covers such a vast range of behavior that it is difficult to believe that a correlation between *any* forms of criminal behavior among peers can be construed as evidence of peer influence. My own position, evident in my research, is that, net of any common source of influence like parents or other mutual associates, the stronger the behavioral similarity between peers (including not only the specific form of behavior but its temporal and spatial pattern as well), the stronger the evidence of influence. My reasoning, which may be wrong, is that theories of peer influence (particularly those that emphasize co-offending) generally provide more reason to anticipate a *close* match between ego and alter's behavior than merely some general similarity or broad common denominator (e.g., "deviant" or "unlawful" behavior).

The most compelling evidence of peer influence would most likely come from studies employing true experimental designs, where subjects are randomly assigned to groups (say, residential units) under controlled circumstances that minimize external influences, and where investigators can measure attitudinal and behavioral convergence among subjects over time and across conditions. This is the approximate design used by the Sherifs (1964), for example, in their study of friendship formation in summer camp dormitories. The logistical and ethical problems of such research are not trivial, however, and they become even more serious when one considers the prospect of placing seriously delinquent youth in the company of other, more conventional youth (though the direction and strength of influence would be a truly fascinating issue). For these reasons, and because of modern constraints on the use of human subjects, such research is unlikely to take place any time soon. One seeming approximation to a true experiment would be to examine youth who enter juvenile or adult detention facilities and observe any changes in their behavior over time. But assignment to such facilities is scarcely a random variable (nor could it be), and the initial composition of the population with respect to the independent variable (deviant behavior or attitudes) is not under the control of the investigator. As is often the case, applying the experimental method to human behavior is not an easy task. Yet such research might help to resolve the most critical questions about the existence and nature of peer influence.

QUALIFICATIONS AND CLARIFICATIONS

The emphasis on peer influence throughout this book may leave the impression that I regard such influence to be the sole cause of crime, or at least the only cause important enough to merit serious attention. Criminologists, to be sure, have always had a penchant for monocausal explanations, and this book may appear to be one more instance of that tendency.

But that characterization mistakes my point of view. The evidence amassed in criminology over the last few decades, I believe, supports the proposition that peer influence is the *principal proximate cause* of most criminal conduct, the last link in what is undoubtedly a longer causal chain. This position does not preclude other explanations of crime (e.g., social inequality, family disruption, social disorganization, severed bonds to conventional institutions), but holds that such variables ultimately affect crime by regulating exposure or susceptibility to delinquent peers (see, for example, Fergusson and Horwood, 1999).

For example, despite the intense historical rivalry between differential association and control theory, the emphasis on the parent/child bond in control theory is well justified by research, in my view, and I concur with Elliott, Huizinga, and Ageton (1985) and others that this bond has a powerful impact on exposure/susceptibility to delinquent peers, and through that channel, on delinquency itself. In all likelihood, the parent/child bond itself is affected by factors like employment status, poverty, family disruption, and (sub)cultural definitions of parenting. The general point is that one cannot look *only* to peers to understand criminal behavior. But social scientists ought to recognize that peers appear to be a vital mediating element in the causal sequence leading up to crime.

I would also concede that there are forms of criminal or deviant behavior that have little to do with peer influence. For example, Tittle and Paternoster (2000) classify types of deviant behavior according to their "sociality," and though they assert that "with few exceptions such as suicide (most of the time) and serial killing, deviance is a group phenomenon" (2000: 397), they also observe (2000: 49) that

> some deviant behavior can be, and almost always is, performed alone; a person doesn't need to be taught how to do it; its practice does not require the cooperation of others; and its continuation does not depend upon emotional and social support from its practitioners.

Aside from suicide and serial killing, Tittle and Paternoster characterize certain apparent forms of mental illness (eating feces, nonsense language) as "individualized" deviance. One might dispute that interpretation by arguing that certain forms of crime and deviance are a consequence of peer *rejection* (see Parker and Asher, 1987; Kupersmidt, Coie, and Dodge, 1990), or by asserting, as Tittle and Paternoster themselves do, that it is the very inability "to relate to others" that gives rise to such behaviors. Yet even were that true, it is simply silly to argue that human beings are incapable of original, solitary, unsocialized behavior, and a theory is strengthened, not weakened, by identifying the class(es) of things or events to which it does *not* apply. In the end, deviant behavior is a country into which there are many roads, even if one may be a highway.

As for the limits of peer explanations, we saw earlier that assault appears to be among the least "groupy" offenses, and there is some reason to believe that, as a class, violent offenses are less often committed by groups than are other offenses. For example, Gold (1970: 86) concludes from his data that "the least companionate acts are impulsive in the degree to which they directly express sexual and aggressive impulses." If this is indeed true, it would not rule out group influence in all violent conduct, and there is good reason to believe that it is vitally important in some situations (see Chapter 4). Nevertheless, it seems clear that the presence of co-offenders is not a *necessary* condition for violence.

In some ways, this idea is not surprising or unexpected. Younger offenders are more likely to operate in groups than older offenders, but it is older offenders who are more likely to engage in violence (e.g., Steffensmeier et al., 1989). Among children, at least, aggressive youngsters are often rejected by their peers (Asher and Coie, 1990; Parkhurst and Asher, 1992). And while many criminal events (including violent ones) seem to result from processes set in motion when groups assemble, violent events also occur when feuding parties chance upon one another in a restroom or bar or at work, or when circumstances bring to life a new grievance or aggravate an old one. In such cases, the onset of conflict is not dependent on the presence of co-*offenders,* though it may well depend on the presence of bystanders or onlookers (see Chapter 4). Unfortunately, although self-report and victimization studies often obtain data on the number of offenders and/or victims present at criminal events, they consistently fail to measure the *total* number of people (including bystanders and other participants) present at those events and the relationships among them. Without data of this kind, it is difficult to decipher the nature of social influence during violent events.

Even when violent offenders act alone, of course, it does not rule out peer influence as an operative element. Individuals may engage in violence in anticipation of the status they stand to gain (or lose) with peers, even if those peers are not present at the moment. (Gold [1970] reports that a sizable proportion of lone offenses reported by adolescents in his survey were quickly recounted to friends.) And whether individuals even recognize or define situations as opportunities for violent crime (e.g., a date as an occasion for rape) can depend on the understandings they have acquired from peers (see Akers, 1998).

FINAL COMMENTS

Through most of the twentieth century, the field of criminology was understood and accepted by academics as a subfield of sociology. The reasons for this seemed clear enough, even to those outside the discipline. Many of the central features of criminal behavior – social class differences, the importance of family and neighborhood, the group nature of delinquency – argued for a sociological approach to the study of crime (e.g., Erickson and Jensen, 1977).

In the late twentieth century, however, investigators from other disciplines – developmental, behavioral, and evolutionary psychology, neurophysiology, and genetics – and even some sociologists raised challenges to the sociological hegemony over the field. Paradigmatic challenges of this sort are not new to criminology, but the evidence and arguments advanced by these challengers were not always trivial or readily dismissible, and when combined with the growing institutional rift between sociology and criminology/criminal justice departments in American universities, they gained ground as in no previous time.

To sociologically oriented criminologists, this new era in criminology has been disorienting and even threatening. What many fail to realize, however, is what a genuine blessing in disguise it truly is. As in any healthy and vibrant science, challenges to orthodox points of view force those who hold such views to reexamine the evidence for their positions and, in so doing, to come to a new appreciation of their own perspective or to concede its weaknesses and accede to a new paradigm.

When it comes to peer influence, this sort of shake-up may be precisely what is needed, for criminologists have often labored under conceptions of peer influence that border on the mystical and that could not possibly bear the weight of close examination. All too often, they have settled for the sorts of everyday adages ("peer pressure," "one bad apple") that populate the English language and are suitable only for afternoons at the pub.

As I have sought to demonstrate in this book, there is every reason to suppose that peer influence is critical to understanding criminal conduct. But the evidence for that argument will ultimately come from

those who are not content to let the issue die, and are willing to under-
take the serious scientific work necessary to settle the question. Even
if the answer proves to be negative, it would put to rest an issue that
has divided criminologists at least since Sutherland's time and has fueled more than a few passionate disputes in the field. As with any truly
good question in science, however, a negative answer would be of no
less value to the field than an affirmative one.

Suggested Readings

Chapter One

Ball, Richard A. and G. David Curry. 1995. "The Logic of Definition in Criminology: Purposes and Methods for Defining 'Gangs.'" *Criminology* 33: 225–245.

Jankowski, Martin S. 1991. *Islands in the Street: Gangs and American Urban Society*. Berkeley: University of California Press.

Kiesler, Charles A. and Sara B. Kiesler. 1970. *Conformity*. Reading, MA: Addison-Wesley.

Klein, Malcolm W. 1969. "On the Group Context of Delinquency." *Sociology and Social Research* 54: 63–71.

Klein, Malcolm W. and Lois Y. Crawford. 1967. "Groups, Gangs, and Cohesiveness." *Journal of Research in Crime and Delinquency* 4: 63–75.

Reiss, Albert J., Jr. 1986. "Co-Offender Influences on Criminal Careers." In Alfred Blumstein, Jacqueline Cohen, Jeffrey Roth, and Christy Visher (eds.), *Criminal Careers and 'Career Criminals.'* Washington, DC: National Academy Press.

Sarnecki, Jerzy. 1986. *Delinquent Networks*. Stockholm: National Council for Crime Prevention.

Shannon, Lyle W. 1991. *Changing Patterns of Delinquency and Crime: A Longitudinal Study in Racine*. Boulder: Westview Press.

Short, James F. 1997. *Poverty, Ethnicity, and Violent Crime*. Boulder: Westview Press.

Thrasher, Frederic M. 1927. *The Gang: A Study of 1,313 Gangs in Chicago.* Chicago: University of Chicago Press.

Warr, Mark. 1990. "Dangerous Situations: Social Context and Fear of Victimization." *Social Forces* 68: 891–907.

Wolfgang, Marvin E., Terence P. Thornberry, and Robert M. Figlio. 1987. *From Boy to Man, from Delinquency to Crime.* Chicago: University of Chicago Press.

Chapter Two

Aries, Philippe. 1962. *Centuries of Childhood: A Social History of Family Life.* Translated by Robert Baldick. New York: Random House.

Berndt, Thomas J. 1979. "Developmental Changes in Conformity to Peers and Parents." *Developmental Psychology* 15: 608–616.

Cairns, Robert B. and Beverly D. Cairns. 1994. *Lifelines and Risks: Pathways of Youth in Our Time.* Cambridge: Cambridge University Press.

Coleman, James S. 1961. *Adolescent Society.* New York: The Free Press.

1974. *Youth: Transition to Adulthood. Report of the Panel on Youth of the President's Science Advisory Committee.* Chicago: University of Chicago Press.

1990. *Foundations of Social Theory.* Cambridge, MA: Harvard University Press.

Coleman, James S. and Thomas Hoffer. 1987. *Public and Private High Schools: The Impact of Communities.* New York: Basic Books.

Crockett, Lisa, Mike Losoff, and Anne C. Petersen. 1984. "Perceptions of the Peer Group and Friendship in Early Adolescence." *Journal of Early Adolescence* 4: 155–181.

Csikszentmihalyi, Mihaly and Reed Larson. 1984. *Being Adolescent: Conflict and Growth in the Teenage Years.* New York: Basic Books.

Devereux, Edward C. 1970. "The Role of Peer-Group Experience in Moral Development." In John P. Hill (ed.), *Minnesota Symposia on Child Development,* Volume 4. Minneapolis: University of Minnesota Press.

Dunphy, Dexter C. 1980. "Peer Group Socialisation." In Rolf E. Muuss (ed.), *Adolescent Behavior and Society: A Book of Readings,* third edition. New York: Random House.

Felson, Marcus. 1994. *Crime and Everyday Life: Insights and Implications.* Thousand Oaks, CA: Pine Forge Press.

Felson, Marcus and Michael Gottfredson. 1984. "Adolescent Activities Near Peers and Parents." *Journal of Marriage and the Family* 46: 709–714.

Gillis, John R. 1974. *Youth and History.* New York: Academic Press.

Greenberg, David. 1985. "Age, Crime, and Social Explanation." *American Journal of Sociology* 91: 1–21.

Hartup, Willard W. 1983. "Peer Relations." In Paul H. Mussen (ed.), *Handbook of Child Psychology. Volume IV: Socialization, Personality, and Social Development.* E. Mavis Hetherington, volume editor. New York: Wiley.

Kandel, Denise B. and Gerald S. Lesser. 1972. *Youth in Two Worlds: United States and Denmark.* San Francisco: Jossey-Bass.

Muuss, Rolf E. 1980. *Adolescent Behavior and Society.* New York: Random House.

Rubin, Kenneth H., William Bukowski, and Jeffrey G. Parker. 1998. "Peer Interactions, Relationships, and Groups." In William Damon (ed.), *Handbook of Child Psychology,* fifth edition. *Volume Three: Social, Emotional, and Personality Development.* New York: Wiley.

Savin-Williams, Ritch C. and Thomas J. Berndt. 1990. "Friendship and Peer Relations." In S. Shirley Feldman and Glen R. Elliott (eds.), *At the Threshold: The Developing Adolescent.* Cambridge, MA: Harvard University Press.

Schlegel, Alice and Herbert Barry III. 1991. *Adolescence: An Anthropological Inquiry.* New York: The Free Press.

Sherif, Muzafer and Carolyn W. Sherif. 1964. *Reference Groups: Exploration into Conformity and Deviation of Adolescents.* New York: Harper and Row.

Steinberg, Laurence D. and Susan B. Silverberg. 1986. "The Vicissitudes of Autonomy in Early Adolescence." *Child Development* 57: 841–851.

Thornburg, Hershel D. 1982. *Development in Adolescence,* second edition. Monterey, CA: Brooks/Cole.

Youniss, James. 1980. *Parents and Peers in Social Development.* Chicago: University of Chicago Press.

Chapter Three

Aseltine, Robert H., Jr. 1995. "A Reconsideration of Parental and Peer Influences on Adolescent Deviance." *Journal of Health and Social Behavior* 36: 103–121.

Briar, Scott and Irving Piliavin. 1965. "Delinquency, Situational Inducements, and Commitment to Conformity." *Social Problems* 13: 35–45.

Elliott, Delbert S. and Scott Menard. 1996. "Delinquent Friends and Delinquent Behavior: Temporal and Developmental Patterns."

In J. David Hawkins (ed.), *Delinquency and Crime: Current Theories.* Cambridge: Cambridge University Press.

Erez, Edna. 1987. "Situational or Planned Crime and the Criminal Career." In Marvin E. Wolfgang, Terence P. Thornberry, and Robert M. Figlio (eds.), *From Boy to Man, from Delinquency to Crime.* Chicago: University of Chicago Press.

Erickson, Maynard L. 1971. "The Group Context of Delinquent Behavior." *Social Problems* 19: 114–129.

Erickson, Maynard L. and Lamar T. Empey. 1965. "Class Position, Peers, and Delinquency." *Sociology and Social Research* 49: 268–282.

Erickson, Maynard L. and Gary F. Jensen. 1977. "Delinquency Is Still Group Behavior!: Toward Revitalizing the Group Premise in the Sociology of Deviance." *Journal of Criminal Law and Criminology* 68: 262–273.

Glueck, Sheldon and Eleanor Glueck. 1950. *Unraveling Juvenile Delinquency.* Cambridge, MA: Harvard University Press.

Gold, Martin. 1970. *Delinquent Behavior in an American City.* Belmont, CA: Brooks/Cole.

Gottfredson, Michael R. and Travis Hirschi. 1990. *A General Theory of Crime.* Stanford, CA: Stanford University Press.

Hepburn, John R. 1977. "Testing Alternative Models of Delinquency Causation." *Journal of Criminal Law and Criminology* 67: 450–460.

Hirschi, Travis. 1969. *Causes of Delinquency.* Berkeley: University of California Press.

Hood, Roger and Richard Sparks. 1970. *Key Issues in Criminology.* New York: McGraw-Hill.

Kandel, Denise B. 1978. "Homophily, Selection, and Socialization in Adolescent Friendships." *American Journal of Sociology* 84: 427–436.

Kornhauser, Ruth R. 1978. *Social Sources of Delinquency: An Appraisal of Analytic Models.* Chicago: University of Chicago Press.

Matsueda, Ross L. 1988. "The Current State of Differential Association Theory." *Crime and Delinquency* 34: 277–306.

Matsueda, Ross L. and Kathleen Anderson. 1998. "The Dynamics of Delinquent Peers and Delinquent Behavior." *Criminology* 36: 269–308.

Miller, Walter B. 1974. "American Youth Gangs: Past and Present." In Abraham S. Blumberg (ed.), *Current Perspectives on Criminal Behavior.* New York: Knopf.

Reiss, Albert J., Jr. and David P. Farrington. 1991. "Advancing Knowledge about Co-Offending: Results from a Prospective Longitudinal Survey of London Males." *Journal of Criminal Law and Criminology* 82: 360–395.

Shaw, Clifford T. and Henry D. McKay. 1931. *Report on the Causes of Crime, Volume II*. Washington, DC: U.S. Government Printing Office.

Thornberry, Terence P., Alan J. Lizotte, Marvin D. Krohn, Margaret Farnworth, and Sung Joon Jang. 1994. "Delinquent Peers, Beliefs, and Delinquent Behavior: A Longitudinal Test of Interactional Theory." *Criminology* 32: 47–84.

Warr, Mark. 1996. "Organization and Instigation in Delinquent Groups." *Criminology* 34: 11–37.

Yablonsky, Lewis. 1959. "The Delinquent Gang as a Near-Group." *Social Problems* 7: 108–117.

Chapter Four

Akers, Ronald L. 1998. *Social Learning and Social Structure: A General Theory of Crime and Deviance*. Boston: Northeastern University Press.

Anderson, Elijah. 1994. "The Code of the Streets." *Atlantic Monthly* 273: 81–94.

1999. *Code of the Street: Decency, Violence, and the Moral Life of the Inner City*. New York: Norton.

Beyth-Marom, Ruth, Laurel Austin, Baruch Fischhoff, Claire Palmgren, and Marilyn Jacobs-Quadrel. 1993. "Perceived Consequences of Risky Behaviors: Adults and Adolescents." *Developmental Psychology* 29: 549–563.

Burgess, Robert and Ronald Akers. 1966. "A Differential Association-Reinforcement Theory of Criminal Behavior." *Social Problems* 14: 128–147.

Caspi, Avshalom, Donald Lynam, Terrie E. Moffitt, and Phil A. Silva. 1993. "Unraveling Girls' Delinquency: Biological, Dispositional, and Contextual Contributions to Adolescent Misbehavior." *Developmental Psychology* 29: 19–30.

Cohen, Lawrence E. and Marcus Felson. 1979. "Social Change and Crime Rate Trends: A Routine Activity Approach." *American Sociological Review* 44: 588–608.

Douvan, Elizabeth and Joseph Adelson. 1966. *The Adolescent Experience*. New York: Wiley.

Eder, Donna. 1991. "The Role of Teasing in Adolescent Peer Group Culture." *Sociological Studies of Child Development* 4: 181–197.

Eder, Donna and Janet Lynne Enke. 1991. "The Structure of Gossip: Opportunities and Constraints on Collective Expression among Adolescents." *American Sociological Review* 56: 494–508.

Eder, Donna and Stephanie Sanford. 1986. "The Development and Maintenance of Interactional Norms among Early Adolescents." In Patricia A. Adler and Peter Adler (eds.), *Sociological Studies of Child Development. Volume One.* Greenwich, CT: JAI Press.

Felson, Richard B. 1993. "Predatory and Dispute-Related Violence: A Social Interactionist Perspective." In Ronald V. Clarke and Marcus Felson (eds.), *Routine Activity and Rational Choice: Advances in Criminological Theory.* New Brunswick, NJ: Transaction.

Festinger, Leon, A. Pepitone, and T. Newcomb. 1952. "Some Consequences of Deindividuation in a Group." *Journal of Abnormal and Social Psychology* 47: 382–389.

Friedkin, Noah E. 1999. "Choice Shift and Group Polarization." *American Sociological Review* 64: 856–875.

Gaylord, Mark S. and John F. Galliher. 1988. *The Criminology of Edwin Sutherland.* New Brunswick, NJ: Transaction Books.

Giordano, Peggy C. 1978. "Girls, Guys and Gangs: The Changing Social Context of Female Delinquency." *Journal of Criminal Law and Criminology* 69: 126–132.

Jensen, Gary F. and Maynard L. Erickson. 1978. "The Social Meaning of Sanctions." In Marvin D. Krohn and Ronald L. Akers (eds.), *Crime, Law, and Sanctions: Theoretical Perspectives.* Beverly Hills, CA: Sage.

Jones, Edward E. 1964. *Ingratiation: A Social Psychological Analysis.* New York: Appleton-Century-Crofts.

LeBon, Gustav. 1895. *Psychologie des Foules.* Paris: Alcan.

Matza, David. 1964. *Delinquency and Drift.* New York: Wiley.

McPhail, Clark. 1991. *The Myth of the Madding Crowd.* New York: Aldine De Gruyter.

Piaget, Jean. 1932. *Le Jugement Moral Chez L'Enfant.* Paris: Librairie Felix Alcan.

Savin-Williams, Richard C. 1980. "An Ethological Study of Dominance Formation and Maintenance in a Group of Human Adolescents." In Rolf E. Muuss (ed.), *Adolescent Behavior and Society: A Book of Readings,* third edition. New York: Random House.

Short, James F. and Fred L. Strodtbeck. 1965. *Group Process and Gang Delinquency.* Chicago: University of Chicago Press.

Simmons, Roberta G. and Dale A. Blyth. 1987. *Moving into Adolescence: The Impact of Pubertal Change and School Context.* New York: Aldine de Gruyter.

Slaby, Ronald G. and Nancy G. Guerra. 1988. "Cognitive Mediators of Aggression in Adolescent Offenders: I. Assessment." *Developmental Psychology* 24: 580–588.

Stattin, H. and D. Magnusson. 1990. *Pubertal Maturation in Female Development.* Hillsdale, NJ: Erlbaum.

Sullivan, Mercer L. 1989. *"Getting Paid": Youth Crime and Work in the Inner City.* Ithaca, NY: Cornell University Press.

Sutherland, Edwin H. 1947. *Principles of Criminology,* fourth edition. Chicago: J. B. Lippincott.

Sykes, Gresham and David Matza. 1957. "Techniques of Neutralization: A Theory of Delinquency." *American Sociological Review* 22: 664–670.

Tonry, Michael and James Q. Wilson. 1990. *Crime and Justice: An Annual Review of Research. Volume 13: Drugs and Crime.* Chicago: University of Chicago Press.

Tremblay, Pierre. 1993. "Searching for Suitable Co-Offenders." In Ronald V. Clarke and Marcus Felson (eds.), *Routine Activity and Rational Choice: Advances in Criminological Theory.* New Brunswick, NJ: Transaction.

Troyer, Lisa and C. Wesley Younts. 1997. "Whose Expectations Matter? The Relative Power of First- and Second-Order Expectations in Determining Social Influence." *American Journal of Sociology* 103: 692–732.

Turner, Ralph H. and Lewis M. Killian. 1987. *Collective Behavior,* third edition. Englewood Cliffs, NJ: Prentice-Hall.

Warr, Mark. 2001. "The Social Origins of Crime: Edwin Sutherland and the Theory of Differential Association." In Raymond Paternoster and Ronet Bachman (eds.), *Explaining Criminals and Crime: Essays in Contemporary Criminological Theory.* Los Angeles: Roxbury.

Warr, Mark and Mark C. Stafford. 1991. "The Influence of Delinquent Peers: What They Think or What They Do?" *Criminology* 29: 851–866.

Chapter Five

Akers, Ronald L. 1992. *Drugs, Alcohol, and Society.* Belmont, CA: Wadsworth.

Bachman, Jerald, Patrick O'Malley, and Lloyd Johnston. 1984. "Drug Use among Young Adults: The Impacts of Role Status and Social Environment." *Journal of Personality and Social Psychology* 47: 629–645.

Blumstein, Alfred and Jaqueline Cohen. 1987. "Characterizing Criminal Careers." *Science* 237: 985–991.

Blumstein, Alfred, Jaqueline Cohen, and David Farrington. 1988. "Criminal Career Research: Its Value for Criminology." *Criminology* 26: 1–35.

Cohen, Lawrence E. and Bryan J. Vila. 1996. "Self-Control and Social Control: An Exposition of the Gottfredson-Hirschi/Sampson-Laub Debate." *Studies on Crime and Crime Prevention* 5: 125–150.

Dishion, Thomas J., Gerald R. Patterson, and Pamela C. Griesler. 1994. "Peer Adaptations in the Development of Antisocial Behavior: A Confluence Model." In L. Rowell Huesmann (ed.), *Aggressive Behavior: Current Perspectives*. New York: Plenum Press.

Elder, Glenn H., Jr. 1985. "Perspectives on the Life Course." In Glenn H. Elder, Jr. (ed.), *Life Course Dynamics*. Ithaca, NY: Cornell University Press.

Elliott, Delbert S., David Huizinga, and Suzanne S. Ageton. 1985. *Explaining Delinquency and Drug Use*. Newbury Park, CA: Sage.

Farrington, David P. 1986. "Age and Crime." In Michael Tonry and Norval Morris (eds.), *Crime and Justice: An Annual Review of Research*. Chicago: University of Chicago Press.

Farrington, David P. and Donald J. West. 1995. "Effects of Marriage, Separation, and Children on Offending by Adult Males." In Zena Smith Blau and John Hagan (eds.), *Current Perspectives on Aging and the Life Cycle. Volume 4: Delinquency and Disrepute in the Life Course*. Greenwich, CT: JAI Press.

Gilligan, Carol. 1982. *In a Different Voice: Psychological Theory and Women's Development*. Cambridge, MA: Harvard University Press.

Hindelang, Michael J., Travis Hirschi, and J. Weis. 1979. "Correlates of Delinquency: The Illusion of Discrepancy between Self-Report and Official Measures." *American Sociological Review* 44: 995–1014.

Hirschi, Travis. 1969. *Causes of Delinquency*. Berkeley: University of California Press.

Hirschi, Travis and Michael R. Gottfredson. 1983. "Age and the Explanation of Crime." *American Journal of Sociology* 89: 553–584.

Jensen, Gary F. 1972. "Parents, Peers, and Delinquent Action: A Test of the Differential Association Perspective." *American Journal of Sociology* 78: 562–575.

Johnson, Richard E. 1979. *Juvenile Delinquency and Its Origins*. Cambridge: Cambridge University Press.

Knight, B. J. and D. J. West. 1975. "Temporary and Continuing Delinquency." *British Journal of Criminology* 15: 43–50.

Matsueda, Ross L. and Karen Heimer. 1997. "A Symbolic Interactionist Theory of Role-Transitions, Role-Commitments, and Delinquency."

In Terence P. Thornberry (ed.), *Developmental Theories of Crime and Delinquency: Advances in Criminological Theory*, Volume 7. New Brunswick, NJ: Transaction.

Mears, Daniel P., Matthew Ploeger, and Mark Warr. 1998. "Explaining the Gender Gap in Delinquency: Peer Influence and Moral Evaluations of Behavior." *Journal of Research in Crime and Delinquency* 35: 251–266.

Sampson, Robert J. and John H. Laub. 1993. *Crime in the Making: Pathways and Turning Points through Life.* Cambridge, MA: Harvard University Press.

Simons, Ronald L., Martin G. Miller, and Stephen M. Aigner. 1980. "Contemporary Theories of Deviance and Female Delinquency: An Empirical Test." *Journal of Research in Crime and Delinquency* 17: 42–53.

Smith, Douglas A. and Raymond Paternoster. 1987. "The Gender Gap in Theories of Deviance: Issues and Evidence." *Journal of Research in Crime and Delinquency* 24: 140–172.

Steffensmeier, Darrell, Emilie Allan, Miles Harer, and Cathy Streifel. 1989. "Age and the Distribution of Crime." *American Journal of Sociology* 94: 803–831.

Thornberry, Terence P. 1997. *Developmental Theories of Crime and Delinquency: Advances in Criminological Theory*, Volume 7. New Brunswick, NJ: Transaction.

Uggen, Christopher. 2000. "Work as a Turning Point in the Life Course of Criminals: A Duration Model of Age, Employment, and Recidivism." *American Sociological Review* 67: 529–546.

Warr, Mark. 1993a. "Age, Peers, and Delinquency." *Criminology* 31: 17–40.
1993b. "Parents, Peers, and Delinquency." *Social Forces* 72: 247–264.
1998. "Life-Course Transitions and Desistance from Crime." *Criminology* 36: 183–216.

Wilson, James Q. and Richard J. Herrnstein. 1985. *Crime and Human Nature.* New York: Simon and Schuster.

Chapter Six

Emler, Nicholas and Stephen Reicher. 1995. *Adolescence and Delinquency: The Collective Management of Reputation.* Oxford: Blackwell.

Fergusson, David M. and L. John Horwood. 1999. "Prospective Childhood Predictors of Deviant Peer Affiliations in Adolescence." *Journal of Child Psychology and Psychiatry* 40: 581–592.

Fuligni, Andrew J. and Jacquelynne S. Eccles. 1993. "Perceived Parent-Child Relationships and Early Adolescents' Orientation toward Peers." *Developmental Psychology* 29: 622–632.

Kupersmidt, Janis B., John D. Coie, and Kenneth A. Dodge. 1990. "The Role of Poor Peer Relationships in the Development of Disorder." In Steven R. Asher and John D. Coie (eds.), *Peer Rejection in Childhood*. Cambridge: Cambridge University Press.

Moffitt, Terrie. 1993. "Adolescence-Limited and Life-Course-Persistent Behavior: A Developmental Taxonomy." *Psychological Review* 100: 674–701.

Parker, Jeffrey G. and Steven R. Asher. 1987. "Peer Relations and Later Personal Adjustment: Are Low-Accepted Children at Risk?" *Psychological Bulletin* 102: 357–389.

Ploeger, Matthew. 1997. "Youth Employment and Delinquency: Reconsidering a Problematic Relationship." *Criminology* 35: 659–675.

Tittle, Charles R. and Raymond Paternoster. 2000. *Social Deviance and Crime: An Organizational and Theoretical Approach*. Los Angeles: Roxbury.

References

Adams, James F. 1973. *Understanding Adolescence: Current Developments in Adolescent Psychology.* Boston: Allyn and Bacon.

Agnew, Robert. 1991. "A Longitudinal Test of Social Control Theory and Delinquency." *Journal of Research in Crime and Delinquency* 28: 126–156.

1994. "The Techniques of Neutralization and Violence." *Criminology* 32: 555–580.

2000. "Sources of Criminality: Strain and Subcultural Theories." In Joseph F. Sheley (ed.), *Criminology: A Contemporary Handbook.* Belmont, CA: Wadsworth.

Akers, Ronald L. 1985. *Deviant Behavior: A Social Learning Approach.* Belmont, CA: Wadsworth.

1992. *Drugs, Alcohol, and Society.* Belmont, CA: Wadsworth.

1998. *Social Learning and Social Structure: A General Theory of Crime and Deviance.* Boston: Northeastern University Press.

Akers, Ronald L., Marvin D. Krohn, Lonn Lanza-Kaduce, and Marcia Radosevich. 1979. "Social Learning and Deviant Behavior: A Specific Test of a General Theory." *American Sociological Review* 44: 636–655.

Anderson, Elijah. 1994. "The Code of the Streets." *Atlantic Monthly* 273: 81–94.

1999. *Code of the Street: Decency, Violence, and the Moral Life of the Inner City.* New York: Norton.

Aries, Philippe. 1962. *Centuries of Childhood: A Social History of Family Life.* Trans. by Robert Baldick. New York: Random House.

Aseltine, Robert H., Jr. 1995. "A Reconsideration of Parental and Peer Influences on Adolescent Deviance." *Journal of Health and Social Behavior* 36: 103–121.

Asher, Steven R. and John D. Coie. 1990. *Peer Rejection in Childhood.* Cambridge: Cambridge University Press.

Ausubel, D. P. 1954. *Theory and Problems of Adolescent Development.* New York: Grune and Stratton, 1954.

Bachman, Jerald, Patrick O'Malley, and Lloyd Johnston. 1984. "Drug Use among Young Adults: The Impacts of Role Status and Social Environment." *Journal of Personality and Social Psychology* 47: 629–645.

Ball, Richard A. and G. David Curry. 1995. "The Logic of Definition in Criminology: Purposes and Methods for Defining 'Gangs.'" *Criminology* 33: 225–245.

Bartusch, Dawn R. Jeglum, Donald R. Lynam, Terrie E. Moffitt, and Phil A. Silva. 1997. "Is Age Important? Testing a General versus a Developmental Theory of Antisocial Behavior." *Criminology* 35: 13–48.

Bem, Daryl J., Michael A. Wallach, and Nathan Kogan. 1965. "Group Decision Making under Risk of Aversive Consequences." *Journal of Personality and Social Psychology* 1: 453–460.

Berger, Joseph, Thomas L. Conner, and M. Hamit Fisek. 1974. *Expectation States Theory: A Theoretical Research Program.* Washington, DC: Winthrop.

Berndt, Thomas J. 1979. "Developmental Changes in Conformity to Peers and Parents." *Developmental Psychology* 15: 608–616.

Beyth-Marom, Ruth, Laurel Austin, Baruch Fischhoff, Claire Palmgren, and Marilyn Jacobs-Quadrel. 1993. "Perceived Consequences of Risky Behaviors: Adults and Adolescents." *Developmental Psychology* 29: 549–563.

Bierstedt, Robert. 1957. *The Social Order.* New York: McGraw-Hill.

Black, Henry C. 1968. *Black's Law Dictionary,* revised fourth edition. St. Paul, MN: West.

Blumer, Herbert. 1939. "Collective Behavior." In Robert E. Park (ed.), *Principles of Sociology.* New York: Barnes and Noble.

Blumstein, Alfred and Jaqueline Cohen. 1987. "Characterizing Criminal Careers." *Science* 237: 985–991.

Blumstein, Alfred, Jaqueline Cohen, and David Farrington. 1988. "Criminal Career Research: Its Value for Criminology." *Criminology* 26: 1–35.

Briar, Scott and Irving Piliavin. 1965. "Delinquency, Situational Inducements, and Commitment to Conformity." *Social Problems* 13: 35–45.

Britt, Chester L. 1994. "Versatility." In Travis Hirschi and Michael R. Gottfredson (eds.), *The Generality of Deviance*. New Brunswick, NJ: Transaction.

Brittain, C. V. 1963. "Adolescent Choices and Parent-Peer Cross-Pressures." *American Sociological Review* 28: 385–391.

Bronfenbrenner, U. 1967. "Response to Pressure from Peers versus Adults among Soviet and American School Children." *International Journal of Psychology* 2: 199–207.

Brown, B. Bradford. 1990. "Peer Groups and Peer Cultures." In S. Shirley Feldman and Glen R. Elliott (eds.), *At the Threshold: The Developing Adolescent*. Cambridge, MA: Harvard University Press.

Burgess, Robert and Ronald Akers. 1966. "A Differential Association-Reinforcement Theory of Criminal Behavior." *Social Problems* 14: 128–147.

Burkett, Steven R. and Bruce O. Warren. 1987. "Religiosity, Peer Influence, and Adolescent Marijuana Use: A Panel Study of Underlying Causal Structures." *Criminology* 25: 109–131.

Bursik, Robert J., Jr. and Harold G. Grasmick. 1993. *Neighborhoods and Crime: The Dimensions of Effective Community Control*. New York: Lexington.

Cairns, Robert B. and Beverly D. Cairns. 1994. *Lifelines and Risks: Pathways of Youth in Our Time*. Cambridge: Cambridge University Press.

Campbell, John D. 1964. "Peer Relations in Childhood." In Martin L. Hoffman and Lois Wladis Hoffman (eds.), *Review of Child Development Research. Volume One*. New York: Russell Sage Foundation.

Caspi, Avshalom, Donald Lynam, Terrie E. Moffitt, and Phil A. Silva. 1993. "Unraveling Girls' Delinquency: Biological, Dispositional, and Contextual Contributions to Adolescent Misbehavior." *Developmental Psychology* 29: 19–30.

Chen, Li-Hui, Susan P. Baker, Elisa R. Braver, and Guohua Li. 2000. "Carrying Passengers as a Risk Factor for Crashes Fatal to 16- and 17-Year-Old Drivers." *Journal of the American Medical Association* 283: 1578–1582.

Cloward, Richard A. and Lloyd E. Ohlin. 1960. *Delinquency and Opportunity: A Theory of Delinquent Gangs*. Glencoe, IL: The Free Press.

Cohen, Albert K. 1955. *Delinquent Boys: The Culture of the Gang*. New York: The Free Press.

Cohen, Bernard P. and Steven D. Silver. 1989. "Group Structure and Information Exchange: Introduction to a Theory." In Joseph Berger, Morris Zelditch, and B. Anderson (eds.), *Sociological Theories in Progress: New Formulations*. Newbury Park, CA: Sage.

Cohen, Lawrence E. and Marcus Felson. 1979. "Social Change and Crime Rate Trends: A Routine Activity Approach." *American Sociological Review* 44: 588–608.

Cohen, Lawrence E. and Bryan J. Vila. 1996. "Self-Control and Social Control: An Exposition of the Gottfredson-Hirschi/Sampson-Laub Debate." *Studies on Crime and Crime Prevention* 5: 125–150.

Coleman, James S. 1961. *Adolescent Society.* New York: The Free Press.

    1974. *Youth: Transition to Adulthood. Report of the Panel on Youth of the President's Science Advisory Committee.* Chicago: University of Chicago Press.

    1990. *Foundations of Social Theory.* Cambridge, MA: Harvard University Press.

Coleman, James S. and Thomas Hoffer. 1987. *Public and Private High Schools: The Impact of Communities.* New York: Basic Books.

Coleman, John C. 1974. *Relationships in Adolescence.* London: Routledge and Kegan Paul.

    1980. "Friendship and the Peer Group in Adolescence." In Joseph Adelson (ed.), *Handbook of Adolescent Psychology.* New York: Wiley.

    1989. "The Focal Theory of Adolescence: A Psychological Perspective." In Klaus Hurrelmann and Uwe Engel (eds.), *The Social World of Adolescents: International Perspectives.* Berlin: Walter de Gruyter.

Conger, John J. and Anne C. Petersen. 1984. *Adolescence and Youth.* New York: Harper and Row.

Costanzo, Philip R. 1980. "Conformity Development as a Function of Self-Blame." In Rolf E. Muuss (ed.), *Adolescent Behavior and Society: A Book of Readings,* third edition. New York: Random House.

Crockett, Lisa, Mike Losoff, and Anne C. Petersen. 1984. "Perceptions of the Peer Group and Friendship in Early Adolescence." *Journal of Early Adolescence* 4: 155–181.

Csikszentmihalyi, Mihaly and Reed Larson. 1984. *Being Adolescent: Conflict and Growth in the Teenage Years.* New York: Basic Books.

Devereux, Edward C. 1970. "The Role of Peer-Group Experience in Moral Development." In John P. Hill (ed.), *Minnesota Symposia on Child Development,* Volume 4. Minneapolis: University of Minnesota Press.

Diener, Edward. 1977. "Deindividuation: Causes and Consequences." *Social Behavior and Personality* 5: 143–155.

    1980. "Deindividuation: The Absence of Self-Awareness and Self-Regulation in Group Members." In Paul B. Paulus (ed.), *Psychology of Group Influence.* Hillsdale, NJ: Erlbaum.

Dipboye, Robert L. 1977. "Alternative Approaches to Deindividuation." *Psychological Bulletin* 84: 1057–1075.

Dishion, Thomas J., Gerald R. Patterson, and Pamela C. Griesler. 1994. "Peer Adaptations in the Development of Antisocial Behavior: A Confluence Model." In L. Rowell Huesmann (ed.), *Aggressive Behavior: Current Perspectives*. New York: Plenum Press.

Dishion, Thomas J., Kathleen M. Spracklen, David W. Andrews, and Gerald R. Patterson. 1996. "Deviancy Training in Male Adolescent Friendships." *Behavior Therapy* 27: 373–390.

Douvan, Elizabeth and Joseph Adelson. 1966. *The Adolescent Experience*. New York: Wiley.

D'Unger, Amy V., Kenneth C. Land, Patricia L. McCall, and Daniel S. Nagin. 1998. "How Many Latent Classes of Delinquent/Criminal Careers? Results from Mixed Poisson Regression Analyses." *American Journal of Sociology* 103: 1593–1630.

Dunphy, Dexter C. 1980. "Peer Group Socialisation." In Rolf E. Muuss (ed.), *Adolescent Behavior and Society: A Book of Readings,* third edition. New York: Random House.

Durkheim, Emile. [1897] 1951. *Suicide.* New York: The Free Press.

Eder, Donna. 1991. "The Role of Teasing in Adolescent Peer Group Culture." *Sociological Studies of Child Development* 4: 181–197.

Eder, Donna and Janet Lynne Enke. 1991. "The Structure of Gossip: Opportunities and Constraints on Collective Expression among Adolescents." *American Sociological Review* 56: 494–508.

Eder, Donna and Stephanie Sanford. 1986. "The Development and Maintenance of Interactional Norms among Early Adolescents." In Patricia A. Adler and Peter Adler (eds.), *Sociological Studies of Child Development. Volume One.* Greenwich, CT: JAI Press.

Elder, Glenn H., Jr. 1985. "Perspectives on the Life Course." In Glenn H. Elder, Jr. (ed.), *Life Course Dynamics.* Ithaca, NY: Cornell University Press.

Elliott, Delbert S., David Huizinga, and Suzanne S. Ageton. 1985. *Explaining Delinquency and Drug Use.* Newbury Park, CA: Sage.

Elliott, Delbert S. and Scott Menard. 1996. "Delinquent Friends and Delinquent Behavior: Temporal and Developmental Patterns." In J. David Hawkins (ed.), *Delinquency and Crime: Current Theories.* Cambridge: Cambridge University Press.

Emler, Nicholas and Stephen Reicher. 1995. *Adolescence and Delinquency: The Collective Management of Reputation.* Oxford: Blackwell.

Empey, Lamar T. 1982. *American Delinquency: Its Meaning and Construction.* Homewood, IL: Dorsey.

Erez, Edna. 1987. "Situational or Planned Crime and the Criminal Career." In Marvin E. Wolfgang, Terence P. Thornberry, and Robert

M. Figlio (eds.), *From Boy to Man, from Delinquency to Crime.* Chicago: University of Chicago Press.

Erickson, Maynard L. 1971. "The Group Context of Delinquent Behavior." *Social Problems* 19: 114–129.

Erickson, Maynard L. and Lamar T. Empey. 1965. "Class Position, Peers, and Delinquency." *Sociology and Social Research* 49: 268–282.

Erickson, Maynard L. and Gary F. Jensen. 1977. "Delinquency Is Still Group Behavior!: Toward Revitalizing the Group Premise in the Sociology of Deviance." *Journal of Criminal Law and Criminology* 68: 262–273.

Erikson, Erik. 1960. "Youth and the Life Cycle." *Children Today* 7: 187–194.

Farrington, David P. 1986. "Age and Crime." In Michael Tonry and Norval Morris (eds.), *Crime and Justice: An Annual Review of Research.* Chicago: University of Chicago Press.

Farrington, David P. and Donald J. West. 1995. "Effects of Marriage, Separation, and Children on Offending by Adult Males." In Zena Smith Blau and John Hagan (eds.), *Current Perspectives on Aging and the Life Cycle. Volume 4: Delinquency and Disrepute in the Life Course.* Greenwich, CT: JAI Press.

Felson, Marcus. 1994. *Crime and Everyday Life: Insights and Implications.* Thousand Oaks, CA: Pine Forge Press.

Felson, Marcus and Michael Gottfredson. 1984. "Adolescent Activities Near Peers and Parents." *Journal of Marriage and the Family* 46: 709–714.

Felson, Richard B. 1993. "Predatory and Dispute-Related Violence: A Social Interactionist Perspective." In Ronald V. Clarke and Marcus Felson (eds.), *Routine Activity and Rational Choice: Advances in Criminological Theory.* New Brunswick, NJ: Transaction.

Fergusson, David M. and L. John Horwood. 1996. "The Role of Adolescent Peer Affiliations in the Continuity between Childhood Behavioral Adjustment and Juvenile Offending." *Journal of Abnormal Child Psychology* 24: 205–221.

1999. "Prospective Childhood Predictors of Deviant Peer Affiliations in Adolescence." *Journal of Child Psychology and Psychiatry* 40: 581–592.

Festinger, Leon, A. Pepitone, and T. Newcomb. 1952. "Some Consequences of Deindividuation in a Group." *Journal of Abnormal and Social Psychology* 47: 382–389.

Festinger, Leon, Stanley Schachter, and Kurt Back. 1950. *Social Pressure in Informal Groups.* New York: Harper and Row.

Friedkin, Noah E. 1999. "Choice Shift and Group Polarization." *American Sociological Review* 64: 856–875.

Fuligni, Andrew J. and Jacquelynne S. Eccles. 1993. "Perceived Parent-Child Relationships and Early Adolescents' Orientation toward Peers." *Developmental Psychology* 29: 622–632.

Gaylord, Mark S. and John F. Galliher. 1988. *The Criminology of Edwin Sutherland.* New Brunswick, NJ: Transaction Books.

Gilligan, Carol. 1982. *In a Different Voice: Psychological Theory and Women's Development.* Cambridge, MA: Harvard University Press.

Gillis, John R. 1974. *Youth and History.* New York: Academic Press.

Giordano, Peggy C. 1978. "Girls, Guys and Gangs: The Changing Social Context of Female Delinquency." *Journal of Criminal Law and Criminology* 69: 126–132.

Giordano, Peggy C., Stephen A. Cernkovich, and M. D. Pugh. 1986. "Friendships and Delinquency." *American Journal of Sociology* 91: 1170–1202.

Glueck, Sheldon and Eleanor Glueck. 1950. *Unraveling Juvenile Delinquency.* Cambridge, MA: Harvard University Press.

Goffman, Erving. 1959. *The Presentation of Self in Everyday Life.* New York: Doubleday.

Gold, Martin. 1970. *Delinquent Behavior in an American City.* Belmont, CA: Brooks/Cole.

Gottfredson, Michael R. and Travis Hirschi. 1988. "Science, Public Policy, and the Career Paradigm." *Criminology* 26: 37–55.

1990. *A General Theory of Crime.* Stanford, CA: Stanford University Press.

Greenberg, David. 1979. "Delinquency and the Age Structure of Society." In David Greenberg (ed.), *Crime and Capitalism: Readings in Marxist Criminology.* Palo Alto, CA: Mayfield.

1985. "Age, Crime, and Social Explanation." *American Journal of Sociology* 91: 1–21.

Grusec, Joan E. and Hugh Lytton. 1988. *Social Development: History, Theory, and Research.* New York: Springer-Verlag.

Guerra, Nancy G., Larry Nucci, and L. Rowell Huesmann. 1994. "Moral Cognition and Childhood Aggression." In L. Rowell Huesmann (ed.), *Aggressive Behavior: Current Perspectives.* New York: Plenum Press.

Hagan, John. 1991. "Destiny and Drift: Subcultural Preferences, Status Attainments, and the Risks and Rewards of Youth." *American Sociological Review* 56: 567–582.

Hartup, Willard W. 1983. "Peer Relations." In Paul H. Mussen (ed.), *Handbook of Child Psychology. Volume IV: Socialization, Personality, and*

Social Development. E. Mavis Hetherington, volume editor. New York: Wiley.

Hawley, Amos. 1950. *Human Ecology: A Theory of Community Structure.* New York: Ronald Press.

Heider, F. 1958. *The Psychology of Interpersonal Relations.* New York: Wiley.

Hepburn, John R. 1977. "Testing Alternative Models of Delinquency Causation." *Journal of Criminal Law and Criminology* 67: 450–460.

Hindelang, Michael J. 1976. "With a Little Help from Their Friends: Group Participation in Reported Delinquency." *British Journal of Criminology* 16: 109–125.

    1979. "Sex Differences in Criminal Activity." *Social Problems* 27: 143–156.

Hindelang, Michael J., Travis Hirschi, and J. Weis. 1979. "Correlates of Delinquency: The Illusion of Discrepancy between Self-Report and Official Measures." *American Sociological Review* 44: 995–1014.

Hirschi, Travis. 1969. *Causes of Delinquency.* Berkeley: University of California Press.

Hirschi, Travis and Michael R. Gottfredson. 1983. "Age and the Explanation of Crime." *American Journal of Sociology* 89: 553–584.

Hoffman, Martin L. 1980. "Moral Development in Adolescence." In Joseph Adelson (ed.), *Handbook of Adolescent Psychology.* New York: Wiley.

Hood, Roger and Richard Sparks. 1970. *Key Issues in Criminology.* New York: McGraw-Hill.

Jankowski, Martin S. 1991. *Islands in the Street: Gangs and American Urban Society.* Berkeley: University of California Press.

Jensen, Gary F. 1969. "'Crime Doesn't Pay': Correlates of a Shared Misunderstanding." *Social Problems* 17: 189–201.

    1972. "Parents, Peers, and Delinquent Action: A Test of the Differential Association Perspective." *American Journal of Sociology* 78: 562–575.

Jensen, Gary F. and David Brownfield. 1983. "Parents and Drugs: Specifying the Consequences of Attachment." *Criminology* 21: 543–554.

Jensen, Gary F. and Maynard L. Erickson. 1978. "The Social Meaning of Sanctions." In Marvin D. Krohn and Ronald L. Akers (eds.), *Crime, Law, and Sanctions: Theoretical Perspectives.* Beverly Hills, CA: Sage.

Johnson, Richard E. 1979. *Juvenile Delinquency and Its Origins.* Cambridge: Cambridge University Press.

Jones, Edward E. 1964. *Ingratiation: A Social Psychological Analysis.* New York: Appleton-Century-Crofts.

Kagan, Jerome and Sharon Lamb. 1987. *The Emergence of Morality in Young Children.* Chicago: University of Chicago Press.

Kandel, Denise B. 1974. "Inter- and Intragenerational Influence on Adolescent Marijuana Use." *Journal of Social Issues* 30: 107–135.

1978. "Homophily, Selection, and Socialization in Adolescent Friendships." *American Journal of Sociology* 84: 427–436.

1996. "The Parental and Peer Contexts of Adolescent Deviance: An Algebra of Interpersonal Influence." *Journal of Drug Issues* 26: 289–315.

Kandel, Denise B. and Gerald S. Lesser. 1969. "Parental and Peer Influences on Educational Plans of Adolescents." *American Sociological Review* 34: 213–223.

1972. *Youth in Two Worlds: United States and Denmark.* San Francisco: Jossey-Bass.

Kandel, Denise B. and Kazuo Yamaguchi. 1987. "Job Mobility and Drug Use: An Event History Analysis." *American Journal of Sociology* 92: 836–878.

Kiesler, Charles A. and Sara B. Kiesler. 1970. *Conformity.* Reading, MA: Addison-Wesley.

Klein, Malcolm W. 1969. "On the Group Context of Delinquency." *Sociology and Social Research* 54: 63–71.

Klein, Malcolm W. and Lois Y. Crawford. 1967. "Groups, Gangs, and Cohesiveness." *Journal of Research in Crime and Delinquency* 4: 63–75.

Klinger, Eric. 1977. *Meaning and Void: Inner Experience and the Incentives in People's Lives.* Minneapolis: University of Minnesota Press.

Knight, B. J. and D. J. West. 1975. "Temporary and Continuing Delinquency." *British Journal of Criminology* 15: 43–50.

Kohlberg, Lawrence. 1964. "Development of Moral Character and Moral Ideology." In Martin L. Hoffman and Lois Wladis Hoffman (eds.), *Review of Child Development Research. Volume One.* New York: Russell Sage Foundation.

1969. "Stage and Sequence: The Cognitive-Developmental Approach to Socialization." In D. A. Goslin (ed.), *Handbook of Socialization Theory and Research.* Chicago: Rand McNally.

Kornhauser, Ruth R. 1978. *Social Sources of Delinquency: An Appraisal of Analytic Models.* Chicago: University of Chicago Press.

Krohn, Marvin D., Alan J. Lizotte, Terence P. Thornberry, Carolyn Smith, and David McDowall. 1996. "Reciprocal Causal Relationships among Drug Use, Peers, and Beliefs: A Five-Wave Panel Model." *Journal of Drug Issues* 26: 405–428.

Kupersmidt, Janis B., John D. Coie, and Kenneth A. Dodge. 1990. "The Role of Poor Peer Relationships in the Development of Disorder." In

Steven R. Asher and John D. Coie (eds.), *Peer Rejection in Childhood.* Cambridge: Cambridge University Press.

Larson, Lyle E. 1980. "The Influence of Parents and Peers during Adolescence: The Situation Hypothesis Revisited." In Rolf E. Muuss (ed.), *Adolescent Behavior and Society: A Book of Readings,* third edition. New York: Random House.

LeBon, Gustav. 1895. *Psychologie des Foules.* Paris: Alcan.

Levine, John M. and Richard L. Moreland. 1990. "Progress in Small Group Research." *Annual Review of Psychology* 41: 585–634.

Lombroso, Caesar and William Ferrero. [1895]1958. *The Female Offender.* New York: Philosophical Press.

Maguire, Kathleen and Ann L. Pastore. 1996. *Sourcebook of Criminal Justice Statistics – 1995.* U.S. Department of Justice, Bureau of Justice Statistics. Washington, DC: U.S. Government Printing Office.

Marcos, Anastasios, Stephen J. Bahr, and Richard E. Johnson. 1986. "Test of a Bonding/Association Theory of Adolescent Drug Use." *Social Forces* 65: 135–161.

Massey, James L. and Marvin D. Krohn. 1986. "A Longitudinal Examination of an Integrated Social Process Model of Deviant Behavior." *Social Forces* 65: 107–134.

Matsueda, Ross L. 1982. "Testing Control Theory and Differential Association: A Causal Modeling Approach." *American Sociological Review* 47: 489–504.

1988. "The Current State of Differential Association Theory." *Crime and Delinquency* 34: 277–306.

Matsueda, Ross L. and Kathleen Anderson. 1998. "The Dynamics of Delinquent Peers and Delinquent Behavior." *Criminology* 36: 269–308.

Matsueda, Ross L. and Karen Heimer. 1987. "Race, Family Structure, and Delinquency: A Test of Differential Association and Social Control Theories." *American Sociological Review* 52: 826–840.

1997. "A Symbolic Interactionist Theory of Role-Transitions, Role-Commitments, and Delinquency." In Terence P. Thornberry (ed.), *Developmental Theories of Crime and Delinquency: Advances in Criminological Theory,* Volume 7. New Brunswick, NJ: Transaction.

Matza, David. 1964. *Delinquency and Drift.* New York: Wiley.

McCarthy, Bill, John Hagan, and Lawrence E. Cohen. 1998. "Uncertainty, Cooperation and Crime: Understanding the Decision to Co-offend." *Social Forces* 77: 155–184.

McPhail, Clark. 1991. *The Myth of the Madding Crowd.* New York: Aldine De Gruyter.

Mears, Daniel P., Matthew Ploeger, and Mark Warr. 1998. "Explaining the Gender Gap in Delinquency: Peer Influence and Moral Evaluations of Behavior." *Journal of Research in Crime and Delinquency* 35: 251–266.

Meeus, Wim. 1989. "Parental and Peer Support in Adolescence." In Klaus Hurrelmann and Uwe Engel (eds.), *The Social World of Adolescents: International Perspectives*. Berlin: Walter de Gruyter.

Meier, Robert F., Steven R. Burkett, and Carol A. Hickman. 1984. "Sanctions, Peers, and Deviance: Preliminary Models of a Social Control Process." *Sociological Quarterly* 25: 67–82.

Miller, Walter B. 1974. "American Youth Gangs: Past and Present." In Abraham S. Blumberg (ed.), *Current Perspectives on Criminal Behavior*. New York: Knopf.

Moffitt, Terrie. 1993. "Adolescence-Limited and Life-Course-Persistent Behavior: A Developmental Taxonomy." *Psychological Review* 100: 674–701.

Morash, Merry. 1983. "Gangs, Groups, and Delinquency." *British Journal of Criminology* 23: 309–331.

Mussen, Paul H., John J. Conger, and Jerome Kagan. 1979. *Child Development and Personality*, fifth edition. New York: Harper and Row.

Muuss, Rolf E. 1980. *Adolescent Behavior and Society*. New York: Random House.

Nagin, Daniel S. and David P. Farrington. 1992a. "The Stability of Criminal Potential from Childhood to Adulthood." *Criminology* 30: 235–260.
   1992b. "The Onset and Persistence of Offending." *Criminology* 30: 501–523.

Nagin, Daniel S. and Kenneth C. Land. 1993. "Age, Criminal Careers, and Population Heterogeneity: Specification and Estimation of a Nonparametric, Mixed Poisson Model." *Criminology* 31: 327–362.

National Institute of Education. 1978. *Violent Schools – Safe Schools: The Safe School Study Report to the Congress, Volume I*. Washington, DC: National Institute of Education.

Nisbett, Richard E., David H. Krantz, Christopher Jepson, and Geoffrey T. Fong. 1982. "Improving Inductive Inference." In Daniel Kahneman, Paul Slovic, and Amos Tversky (eds.), *Judgment under Uncertainty: Heuristics and Biases*. Cambridge: Cambridge University Press.

O'Brien, Robert M. 1995. "Crime and Victimization Data." In Joseph F. Sheley (ed.), *Criminology: A Contemporary Handbook*. Belmont, CA: Wadsworth.

Parker, Jeffrey G. and Steven R. Asher. 1987. "Peer Relations and Later Personal Adjustment: Are Low-Accepted Children at Risk?" *Psychological Bulletin* 102: 357–389.

Parkhurst, Jennifer T. and Steven R. Asher. 1992. "Peer Rejection in Middle School: Subgroup Differences in Behavior, Loneliness, and Interpersonal Concerns." *Developmental Psychology* 28: 231–241.

Paternoster, Raymond. 1988. "Examining Three-Wave Deterrence Models: A Question of Temporal Order and Specification." *Journal of Criminal Law and Criminology* 79: 135–179.

Paternoster, Raymond and Robert Brame. 1997. "Multiple Routes to Delinquency? A Test of Developmental and General Theories of Crime." *Criminology* 35: 49–80.

Paternoster, Raymond and Sally Simpson. 1993. "A Rational Choice Theory of Corporate Crime." In Ronald V. Clarke and Marcus Felson (eds.), *Routine Activity and Rational Choice: Advances in Criminological Theory*. New Brunswick, NJ: Transaction.

Patterson, Gerald R. and Thomas J. Dishion. 1985. "Contributions of Families and Peers to Delinquency." *Criminology* 23: 63–79.

Perlmutter, Rosanne and Ester R. Shapiro. 1987. "Morals and Values in Adolescence." In Vincent B. Van Hasselt and Michel Hersen (eds.), *Handbook of Adolescent Psychology*. New York: Permagon.

Piaget, Jean. 1932. *Le Jugement Moral Chez L'Enfant*. Paris: Librairie Felix Alcan.

Ploeger, Matthew. 1997. "Youth Employment and Delinquency: Reconsidering a Problematic Relationship." *Criminology* 35: 659–675.

Polansky, N., R. Lippitt, and F. Redl. 1950. "An Investigation of Behavioral Contagion in Groups." *Human Relations* 3: 319–348.

Reed, Mark D. and Pamela Wilcox Rountree. 1997. "Peer Pressure and Adolescent Substance Use." *Journal of Quantitative Criminology* 13: 143–180.

Reiss, Albert J., Jr. 1986. "Co-Offender Influences on Criminal Careers." In Alfred Blumstein, Jacqueline Cohen, Jeffrey Roth, and Christy Visher (eds.), *Criminal Careers and 'Career Criminals.'* Washington, DC: National Academy Press.

Reiss, Albert J., Jr. and David P. Farrington. 1991. "Advancing Knowledge about Co-Offending: Results from a Prospective Longitudinal Survey of London Males." *Journal of Criminal Law and Criminology* 82: 360–395.

Reiss, Albert J., Jr. and A. Lewis Rhodes. 1964. "An Empirical Test of Differential Association Theory." *Journal of Research in Crime and Delinquency* 1: 5–18.

Ridgeway, Cecilia L. and James W. Balkwell. 1997. "Group Processes and the Diffusion of Status-Beliefs." *Social Psychology Quarterly* 60: 14–31.

Ross, L. 1977. "The Intuitive Psychologist and His Shortcomings: Distortions in the Attribution Process." In Leonard Berkowitz (ed.), *Advances in Experimental Social Psychology*, Volume 10. New York: Academic Press.

Rubin, Kenneth H., William Bukowski, and Jeffrey G. Parker. 1998. "Peer Interactions, Relationships, and Groups." In William Damon (ed.), *Handbook of Child Psychology*, fifth edition. *Volume Three: Social, Emotional, and Personality Development*. New York: Wiley.

Sampson, Robert J. and W. Byron Groves. 1989. "Community Structure and Crime: Testing Social-Disorganization Theory." *American Journal of Sociology* 94: 774–802.

Sampson, Robert J. and John H. Laub. 1993. *Crime in the Making: Pathways and Turning Points through Life*. Cambridge, MA: Harvard University Press.

Sarnecki, Jerzy. 1986. *Delinquent Networks*. Stockholm: National Council for Crime Prevention.

Savin-Williams, Richard C. 1980. "An Ethological Study of Dominance Formation and Maintenance in a Group of Human Adolescents." In Rolf E. Muuss (ed.), *Adolescent Behavior and Society: A Book of Readings*, third edition. New York: Random House.

Savin-Williams, Ritch C. and Thomas J. Berndt. 1990. "Friendship and Peer Relations." In S. Shirley Feldman and Glen R. Elliott (eds.), *At the Threshold: The Developing Adolescent*. Cambridge, MA: Harvard University Press.

Schlegel, Alice and Herbert Barry III. 1991. *Adolescence: An Anthropological Inquiry*. New York: The Free Press.

Schwartz, Gary. 1987. *Beyond Conformity or Rebellion: Youth and Authority in America*. Chicago: University of Chicago Press.

Shannon, Lyle W. 1988. *Criminal Career Continuity: Its Social Context*. New York: Human Sciences Press.

　　1991. *Changing Patterns of Delinquency and Crime: A Longitudinal Study in Racine*. Boulder: Westview Press.

Shaw, Clifford T. 1931. *The Natural History of a Delinquent*. Chicago: University of Chicago Press.

Shaw, Clifford T. and Henry D. McKay. 1931. *Report on the Causes of Crime, Volume II*. Washington, DC: U.S. Government Printing Office.

Shaw, Marvin E. 1981. *Group Dynamics: The Psychology of Small Group Behavior*. New York: McGraw-Hill.

Sherif, Muzafer and Carolyn W. Sherif. 1964. *Reference Groups: Exploration into Conformity and Deviation of Adolescents*. New York: Harper and Row.

Short, James F. 1957. "Differential Association and Delinquency." *Social Problems* 4: 233–239.

1969. "Social Structure and Group Processes in Explanations of Gang Delinquency." In Muzafer Sherif and Carolyn W. Sherif (eds.), *Problems of Youth: Transition to Adulthood in a Changing World.* Chicago: Aldine.

1990. *Delinquency and Society.* Englewood Cliffs, NJ: Prentice-Hall.

1997. *Poverty, Ethnicity, and Violent Crime.* Boulder: Westview Press.

Short, James F. and Fred L. Strodtbeck. 1965. *Group Process and Gang Delinquency.* Chicago: University of Chicago Press.

Simmons, Roberta G. and Dale A. Blyth. 1987. *Moving into Adolescence: The Impact of Pubertal Change and School Context.* New York: Aldine de Gruyter.

Simons, Ronald L., Christine Johnson, Rand D. Conger, and Glen Elder, Jr. 1998. "A Test of Latent Trait Versus Life-Course Perspectives on the Stability of Adolescent Antisocial Behavior." *Criminology* 36: 217–243.

Simons, Ronald L., Martin G. Miller, and Stephen M. Aigner. 1980. "Contemporary Theories of Deviance and Female Delinquency: An Empirical Test." *Journal of Research in Crime and Delinquency* 17: 42–53.

Simons, Ronald L., Chyi-In Wu, Rand D. Conger, and Frederick O. Lorenz. 1994. "Two Routes to Delinquency: Differences between Early and Late Starters in the Impact of Parenting and Deviant Peers." *Criminology* 32: 247–275.

Slaby, Ronald G. and Nancy G. Guerra. 1988. "Cognitive Mediators of Aggression in Adolescent Offenders: I. Assessment." *Developmental Psychology* 24: 580–588.

Smith, Douglas A. and Raymond Paternoster. 1987. "The Gender Gap in Theories of Deviance: Issues and Evidence." *Journal of Research in Crime and Delinquency* 24: 140–172.

Snow, David A. and Ronnelle Paulsen. 1992. "Crowds and Riots." In Edgar F. Borgatta and Marie L. Borgatta (eds.), *Encyclopedia of Sociology.* New York: Macmillan.

Stafford, Mark C. 1984. "Gang Delinquency." In Robert F. Meier (ed.), *Major Forms of Crime.* Beverly Hills, CA: Sage.

Stattin, H. and D. Magnusson. 1990. *Pubertal Maturation in Female Development.* Hillsdale, NJ: Erlbaum.

Steffensmeier, Darrell and Emilie Allan. 1995. "Criminal Behavior: Gender and Age." In Joseph F. Sheley (ed.), *Criminology: A Contemporary Handbook.* Belmont, CA: Wadsworth.

Steffensmeier, Darrell, Emilie Allan, Miles Harer, and Cathy Streifel. 1989. "Age and the Distribution of Crime." *American Journal of Sociology* 94: 803–831.

Steinberg, Laurence D. and John P. Hill. 1980. "Family Interaction Patterns during Early Adolescence." In Rolf E. Muuss (ed.), *Adolescent Behavior and Society: A Book of Readings,* third edition. New York: Random House.

Steinberg, Laurence D. and Susan B. Silverberg. 1986. "The Vicissitudes of Autonomy in Early Adolescence." *Child Development* 57: 841–851.

Sullivan, Mercer L. 1989. *"Getting Paid": Youth Crime and Work in the Inner City.* Ithaca, NY: Cornell University Press.

Sutherland, Edwin H. 1937. *The Professional Thief.* Chicago: University of Chicago Press.

1939. *Principles of Criminology,* third edition. Chicago: J. B. Lippincott.

1947. *Principles of Criminology,* fourth edition. Chicago: J. B. Lippincott.

Sykes, Gresham and David Matza. 1957. "Techniques of Neutralization: A Theory of Delinquency." *American Sociological Review* 22: 664–670.

Theodorson, George A. and Achilles G. Theodorson. 1979. *A Modern Dictionary of Sociology.* New York: Barnes and Noble.

Thornburg, Hershel D. 1982. *Development in Adolescence,* second edition. Monterey, CA: Brooks/Cole.

Thornberry, Terence P. 1987. "Toward an Interactional Theory of Delinquency." *Criminology* 25: 863–891.

1997. *Developmental Theories of Crime and Delinquency: Advances in Criminological Theory,* Volume 7. New Brunswick, NJ: Transaction.

Thornberry, Terence P., Alan J. Lizotte, Marvin D. Krohn, Margaret Farnworth, and Sung Joon Jang. 1994. "Delinquent Peers, Beliefs, and Delinquent Behavior: A Longitudinal Test of Interactional Theory." *Criminology* 32: 47–84.

Thrasher, Frederic M. 1927. *The Gang: A Study of 1,313 Gangs in Chicago.* Chicago: University of Chicago Press.

Tittle, Charles R., Mary Jean Burke, and Elton F. Jackson. 1986. "Modeling Sutherland's Theory of Differential Association: Toward an Empirical Clarification." *Social Forces* 65: 405–432.

Tittle, Charles R. and Raymond Paternoster. 2000. *Social Deviance and Crime: An Organizational and Theoretical Approach.* Los Angeles: Roxbury.

Tonry, Michael and James Q. Wilson. 1990. *Crime and Justice: An Annual Review of Research. Volume 13: Drugs and Crime.* Chicago: University of Chicago Press.

Tremblay, Pierre. 1993. "Searching for Suitable Co-Offenders." In Ronald V. Clarke and Marcus Felson (eds.), *Routine Activity and Rational Choice: Advances in Criminological Theory.* New Brunswick, NJ: Transaction.

Troyer, Lisa and C. Wesley Younts. 1997. "Whose Expectations Matter? The Relative Power of First- and Second-Order Expectations in Determining Social Influence." *American Journal of Sociology* 103: 692–732.

Turiel, Elliot. 1983. *The Development of Social Knowledge: Morality and Convention.* Cambridge: Cambridge University Press.

Turner, Ralph H. and Lewis M. Killian. 1987. *Collective Behavior,* third edition. Englewood Cliffs, NJ: Prentice-Hall.

Uggen, Christopher. 2000. "Work as a Turning Point in the Life Course of Criminals: A Duration Model of Age, Employment, and Recidivism." *American Sociological Review* 67: 529–546.

United States Departments of Education and Justice. 1999. *1999 Annual Report on School Safety.* Washington, DC: U.S. Departments of Education and Justice.

Vold, George B. and Thomas J. Bernard. 1986. *Theoretical Criminology,* third edition. Oxford: Oxford University Press.

Voss, Harwin L. 1964. "Differential Association and Reported Delinquency Behavior: A Replication." *Social Problems* 12: 78–85.

Wallach, Michael A., Nathan Kogan, and Daryl J. Bem. 1962. "Group Influence on Individual Risk Taking." *Journal of Abnormal Social Psychology* 65: 75–86.

1964. "Diffusion of Responsibility and Level of Risk Taking in Groups." *Journal of Abnormal Social Psychology* 68: 263–274.

Warr, Mark. 1989. "What is the Perceived Seriousness of Crimes?" *Criminology* 27: 795–821.

1990. "Dangerous Situations: Social Context and Fear of Victimization." *Social Forces* 68: 891–907.

1993a. "Age, Peers, and Delinquency." *Criminology* 31: 17–40.

1993b. "Parents, Peers, and Delinquency." *Social Forces* 72: 247–264.

1994. "Public Perceptions and Reactions to Violent Offending and Victimization." In Albert J. Reiss, Jr. and Jeffrey A. Roth (eds.), *Understanding and Preventing Violence. Volume IV: Consequences and Control.* Washington, DC: National Academy Press.

1996. "Organization and Instigation in Delinquent Groups." *Criminology* 34: 11–37.

1998. "Life-Course Transitions and Desistance from Crime." *Criminology* 36: 183–216.

2000. "Fear of Crime in the United States: Avenues for Research and Policy." In David Duffee (ed.), *Criminal Justice 2000. Volume Four: Measurement and Analysis of Crime and Justice.* Washington, DC: U.S. Department of Justice, National Institute of Justice.

2001. "The Social Origins of Crime: Edwin Sutherland and the Theory of Differential Association." In Raymond Paternoster and Ronet Bachman (eds.), *Explaining Criminals and Crime: Essays in Contemporary Criminological Theory.* Los Angeles: Roxbury.

2002. "Crime and Opportunity: A Theoretical Essay." Forthcoming in William Laufer and Freda Adler (series editors), *Advances in Criminological Theory. Volume IX: The Process and Structure of Crime: Criminal Events and Crime Analysis,* edited by Robert Meier, Leslie Kennedy, and Vincent Sacco. New Brunswick, NJ: Transaction.

Warr, Mark and Mark C. Stafford. 1991. "The Influence of Delinquent Peers: What They Think or What They Do?" *Criminology* 29: 851–866.

Webster, Murray, Jr. and Stuart J. Hysom. 1998. "Creating Status Characteristics." *American Sociological Review* 63: 351–378.

Wilson, James Q. and Richard J. Herrnstein. 1985. *Crime and Human Nature.* New York: Simon and Schuster.

Wilson, Monica. 1963. *Good Company: A Study of Nyakyusa Age-Villages.* Boston: Beacon Press.

Wolfgang, Marvin E., Terence P. Thornberry, and Robert M. Figlio. 1987. *From Boy to Man, from Delinquency to Crime.* Chicago: University of Chicago Press.

Yablonsky, Lewis. 1959. "The Delinquent Gang as a Near-Group." *Social Problems* 7: 108–117.

Youniss, James. 1980. *Parents and Peers in Social Development.* Chicago: University of Chicago Press.

Youniss, James and Jacqueline Smollar. 1985. *Adolescent Relations with Mothers, Fathers, and Friends.* Chicago: University of Chicago Press.

Zimbardo, Phillip. 1969. "Individuation, Reason and Order vs. Deindividuation, Impulse, and Chaos." In W. J. Arnold and D. Levine (eds.), *Nebraska Symposium on Motivation,* Volume 17. Lincoln: University of Nebraska Press.

Index